BEE HILL RIVER MAN

Kandulangu-bidi

BEE HILL RIVER MAN
Kandulangu-bidi

Memories of Jack McPhee

Jack McPhee
Patricia Konigsberg

Magabala Books

First published by Magabala Books Aboriginal Corporation,
Broome, Western Australia, 1994

Magabala Books receives financial assistance from the State Government of Western Australia
through the Department for the Arts; the Aboriginal and Torres Strait Islander Commission;
and the Aboriginal and Torres Strait Islander Arts Committee of the Australia Council, the
Federal Government's arts funding and advisory body

Designer Narelle Jones
Editor Rachel Bin Salleh
Advisory Editor Peter Bibby
Production Grant Drage
Printed by Griffin Press, Adelaide, South Australia
Typeset in 11/13pt New Century

National Library of Australia
Cataloguing-in-Publication data:

McPhee, Jack and Konigsberg, Patricia
Bee Hill River Man
Kandulangu-bidi
Memories of Jack McPhee.

Bibliography.
ISBN 1 875641 14 9.

1. McPhee, Jack. [2.] Aborigines, Australian – Western
Australia – Biography. [3.] Aborigines, Australian – Western
Australia – Social life and customs. [4.] Aboriginal Australian
stockmen – Western Australia – Biography. [5.] Nyamal
(Australian people) – Biography. I. Title.

994.10049915

Cover photograph: Louis Warren
Design: Sam Cook and Narelle Jones

In memory of all those who have gone.
Kandulangu, Bee Hill River, that's the Davis River.
That's my family. That's where the tribe comes from. Bidi,
that's where he belongs to. Kandulangu-bidi, that's this book.

Jack McPhee

Acknowledgements

I would like to thank my good friends from Port Hedland, Marble Bar and Nullagine, who over the years have supported and encouraged me: Alan Dwyer, Bidgie and Jean Walsh, John Bailey and wife, Lawrence Emery, Dennis O'Meara, Len Lever, Dr Don Wilson, Dr Grey, Ian Blair, Kaye Richardson, Betty Hagin and Kathleen and Heather Hillary. Thanks to Louis Warren for photographic and other help.

I would also like to thank the following Aboriginal people who have stood by me, backed me up, and encouraged me to keep going. My grandaughters Denise Powdrill, Joanne McPhee and Sally Morgan. Billy Murphy, Mannie Lockyer, Vincent and Jerry Clarke and Septu Midi.

Jack McPhee

I would like to thank the following people: Priscilla Clayton and Pat Gallaher of the Geraldton Public Library for the time and effort put into researching the accuracy of station owners and other personailties mentioned in the book; the Department of Land Administration, Geographic Names Subsection, Brian Goodchild, June Gronow and in particular Ian Elliot for his research into place names; Noelene Holmes from the Meekatharra Shire Council for her help, Diana MacCallum from the Wangka Maya Pilbara Aboriginal Language Centre for her advice on standardisation of a Nyamal spelling system and Prue Timpson-Wearne of Hamersley Iron for allowing me to use the map of gold mines in the Pilbara. Thanks to Des Moloney from Hedland Emporium for his contribution of historical photographs.

My thanks also go to my loving husband, Michael Aylward Smith, for his patience, motivation, his background knowledge of Aboriginal history of the Pilbara, and geography, as well as his editorial help; my mother and sisters, Ingrid and Jeanine, for their encouragement and love.

Patricia Konigsberg

Contents

List of illustrations   *viii*

Foreword   *ix*

Orthography   *xi*

Prologue   Nobody had money   1

Chapter

1	That's how my name come to be McPhee	3
2	There's a dead man here	9
3	So I got a brainwash	17
4	Chasing brumby horses	27
5	Out bush	36
6	Horses, camels and donkeys but no money	52
7	She's half round, half square and crooked	60
8	Down the Murchison (1927-1931)	74
9	There is a story	86
10	Not for the love of money	98
11	That was the true story	104
12	They never came home	128
13	You took what you could get	133
14	After the strike	139
15	Recognition at last	143
16	Old class, old people	148

Glossary, Aboriginal place names   *155*

Maps

Stations, Pilbara to Broome   *43*

Some Pilbara mine workings   *115*

Pilbara and Gascoyne stations   *154*

Nyamal country: English place names and Nyamal translations — rear foldout

Metric equivalents   *158*

Further reading   *159*

Index   *160*

List of illustrations

First group:

37   Jack McPhee, 1930s

38-9   Pearling luggers at the Hedland jetty

40a   Port Headland creek (and street) running a banker, cyclone 1939

40b   Port Hedland and foreshore in the 1930s

41a   Taplin's garage and truck fleet, Port Hedland 1930s

41a   Port Hedland in the 1930s

42   Dr Ed Vines' grave at Braeside Station. Photo P. Konigsberg

44a   Draught camel team and two-wheeler carting wool, Limestone Station

44b   T-model Ford in work, 1930s

Second group:

109   Jack McPhee 1994. Photo Louis Warren

111-12 Draught camel team and dray carting wool at Corunna (?) Station. Photo E.L. Mitchell

11a   Billy McKenna and family getting water, daughter at the windlass handle, government well, Port Hedland. Dad worked hard

11b   Mick Blair yandying for tin, Moolyella strike

113a   Paddling tin at Moolyella 1904

113b   The Thompsons, Marble bar

114a   Port Hedland from the air, 1930s

114b   Pilbara. Photo P. Konigsberg

116   Frank Welsh and Jack McPhee 1985. Photo Dennis O'Meara

Foreword

I first met Jack McPhee while working at Pundulmurra
College. This came about when I was asked to record some
Ngarla/Nyamal corroborees so they could be passed on to
the younger people of that group. Having originally come to
Australia with the thought of pursuing linguistic work on
Aboriginal languages, I was extremely pleased when I was
introduced to Jack McPhee as an acknowledged authority
on the little researched Nyamal Language. From then on I
saw Jack on a weekly basis, having chats and recording
Nyamal words and sentences in order to study the structure
of the language.

As Jack illustrated the differences of words in use of
languages up and down the Oakover River, interspersed
with anecdotes of his life, he became more and more preoc-
cupied with putting these stories into a book in his own
words. In time the importance of such a project became so
essential to him that the linguistic work finally gave way to
the story work.

Armed with my tape recorder and a box of tapes, I began the easy part, that is, to record Jack's stories. When Jack began to relive his past, the urge to return to visit his home country became stronger. This resulted in a trip to Warrawagine, Braeside and the area of Running Waters and Skull Springs – in search for the tree under which his mother and aunty delivered Mrs Hodgson's baby, as well as other places of significance to him in that area. On return this meant more stories and more detailed versions of stories told earlier.

Once the tapes were transcribed, came the difficult task of researching and verifying names and places mentioned and editing stories which sometimes had been told up to four times in varying degrees of detail. The book is written verbatim, in the belief that oral literature has a place in the printed form. I am most grateful to Jack's grandaughter, Denise Powdrill, for transcribing and typing the stories.

Another time consuming challenge was the preparation of the map which Jack wanted included in his book. All place names (for example rivers, creeks and rockholes) had to be translated; a practice that, in my opinion, should be exercised Australia-wide, where access to names is still available and authentic.

The contribution of Aboriginal pastoral workers to the development of the stations of the north of Western Australia has never been fully recognised. Through his anecdotes, Jack gives an insight into the characters and conditions of the time from an Aboriginal working man's perspective and traces the non-Aboriginal settlement of Nyamal land on the Oakover, from the coast to the desert — from De Grey Station to Braeside. Stories about his time "outside" this area in places such as the Kimberley, the Murchison and the Metropolitan area are included as they represent significant events in his life.

Finally, the litany of station owners and water places is extremely important as attention to detail of this type ensures the accurate oral transmission of stories in tradition as they are sung in a corroboree, the cultural common form of passing knowledge through generations.

Patricia Konigsberg

Orthography

This spelling system is a guide to pronouncing Nyamal words.

a as in dark
aa same as *a* but longer
b as in bullet
d as in dam
g as in gun
i as in tin
ii same as *i* but longer
j as in jug
k as in king
l like English *l*
lh made by saying *l* with your tongue blade pressed against the back of your top front teeth
m like English *m*
n like English *n*
ng as in sing
nh made by saying *n* with your tongue blade pressed against the back of your top front teeth

p as in pound
r as in English run
rl like *l* said with the tongue tip curled backwards
rn like *n* said with the tongue tip curled backwards
rr a trilled *r* like in Italian or Scottish English
rt like *d* said with the tongue tip curled backwards
t as in tale
th made with your tongue blade pressed against the back of your top front teeth, like a *th* sound in English
u as in put
uu same as *u* but longer
w like English *w*
y as in yellow

Linguistic note

The spelling is not standardised. Although voicing is generally not distinctive in Aboriginal languages, I have decided to keep all six plosives, the voiced b, d, g and the voiceless p, t, k, as little research has been made into Nyamal and these distinctions seem important to Jack.

Prologue

Nobody had money
Hedland harbour jetty, 1911

We'll start off the proper way. We'll start off at the Hedland jetty. The name for that is Marapikurinha — that's the Aboriginal name. In English it's Hedland Harbour Jetty.

When I first came to Port Hedland in 1911, I saw two ships. That's the first two I've seen in my life — I was only little, you know. That was the *Bullara* and the *Koombana*. The *Bullara* pulled into the jetty and unloaded. She didn't have much cargo on and she went out on the same tide, and the *Koombana* stayed overnight. That was because she was a big ship. A big cattle ship. She was a pretty ship. She didn't go out until the next day at eleven o'clock, when the tide went out, you know. I was only down there for a quick visit on the train that time but I came back in 1913 and 1914 for my father Sandy McPhee.

On the way from Port Hedland to Marble Bar, there was three hotels; one up here, and Poondina on Petermarer Creek, that's twenty-four miles from here; and then Coongan pub, which must've been something like twenty-four miles too. There was another hotel there on Gorge Creek after Carlindie. The train went through Eginbah to Marble Bar. The train went through in 1908, and they stopped it in 1952. That's when they started transport in trucks. They said the government couldn't keep it going for some unknown reason. I've had many rides on that train. It did alright. The fare was a quid from Port Hedland to Marble Bar or Marble Bar to Port Hedland; a quid, that's a pound.

Alex McKinnon, he was the engine driver. He used to drive the loco, old Alex, and there was Frank Trembath, he was the guard on the train.

In Port Hedland, there was a shortage of water and every house had only brackish water until the train came through. The train used to cart the water as far as Eginbah, Shaw River and Poondino on big round tanks. People used to get the water from the railway station with horse and cart and a hundred gallon tank, that was for drinking. The town was small then, only one butcher shop, four pubs and three Chinaman stores. There was Aug Qua, Ho Tong Fatt, Ah Boon, Ah Tow, Zuki, Souey and Quansing. That was the Chinamans that had the shops. Everything was cheap, it had to be, nobody had money.

Out at the Four Mile there is a place where you can get the best cool fresh water. There is a government well there too. That water was much better than the water you'd get in town. You couldn't really take much away because it's only a little hole. I don't know how deep it was, but it was real beautiful water. The further you get away from the coast, the water got better.

That's how my name come to be McPhee

Memories from the old people

See, my mother, her name was Mary Anne Bandijim. She was working for my real father, Bert Watson. He owned a pub and a store — groceries, tucker and all that sorta thing — at Moolyella. She was there for quite a while before I was born. Her sister Dinah Carpenter also worked for this storekeeper. He had a store and a pub, a hotel. On the twenty-fifth of November 1905 I was born. My mother went to work about three days after I was born, with a wooden cradle, a tadu, they call them. This is what they tell me. So, the storekeeper said, "What have you got there, Mary Bandijim?"

"Oh, I got this boy, he belong to you."

"Oh no, I don't want him, take him away. I don't want him and you can go too, don't come back here anymore!"

That was my real father. He was a married man. He had a few kids. I don't know how many in the family. They were down in Perth, Guildford somewhere. He didn't want them to know anything about it. So my mother had to go and battle getting tin. She found a good little patch, got some spinifex and made a shade for me and put me under there. There's plenty of tin those days, but it was cheap, only about two and six a pound in those days.

So Sandy McPhee come along. He was working tin too, but dry-blowing. He knew my mother because she'd been working at the store and he was coming to the store to do the shopping. He said, "Hello Mary! What are you doing here?"

She said, "Oh Bert Watson kicked me out."

"What for?"

"Because I got that little fella. He belong to him."

"Oh, did he? Well, I'll tell you what I'll do. I take you and the baby too."

That's how my name come to be McPhee — because I wasn't wanted by my real father. That was in 1905, 25th November. Sandy McPhee kept us, reared me up and looked after my mother until she died. I was only about three to four years old then. I was too young, the old man couldn't look after me. My Aunty Eva looked after me until the police came.

We were at Moolyella then, I was there as a kid. Well, they used to tell us a lot of stories, you know. Tell us stories that'd frighten us; not to go in the bush on your own at night and all that sorta thing.

Pidadepina

"There was two women, two sisters they were. They used to roam around on their own, very pretty these two girls were, very pretty, so I believe, according to the old people. They had no man, they never seen a man before. These two girls used to wander around, nothing to worry them. They used to live on their own, they had no clothes on of course, there was no such things as clothes. They camped at Nilguna, that's a pool.

4

A man, a black man, came from somewhere. He was looking for a rockhole and he seen a fire, just after dark. He walked over close to the fire and he sung out. He didn't know who was there. They answered him and they asked him who he was and he told them, "I'm Pidadepina," only in Aboriginal language: Pidadepina. The two girls asked him, "What are you, Karimarra or Purungu?" He said, "Purungu."[1]

"Oh well, we are Karimarra, you better stop there. We tua[2] to you!" So he did, he stayed there. According to the custom, they could talk to one another, but they couldn't come close to one another.

He went back on the track of these two girls. He followed them across the Oakover River. They're only just in front of him all the time, but he couldn't catch up to them. They made a camp near a place called Tooma, big waterhole there. When he caught up, they told him, "That's your camp and this our camp. You can't leave that place, you can't come here."

"Okay."

So they made a decent sorta camp with firebreak. They used to sleep together, these two sisters. This fella, he stopped back a bit and made his camp and stayed. He made a fire. He lay there for about two minutes. Ants bothered him, they started biting him. He was hunting them away. He couldn't rest. So, he sung out to those two sisters and they said, "Well come this way a little bit — not far — you might be camped on a ants' nest."

So he came there. It was just the same. The ants wouldn't leave him alone, he reckoned. "Come a bit closer. There might be nothing there." He wasn't supposed to come close, but he came closer. It was just as bad there. In fact, the ants were worse. He lay there for a while, but the ants annoyed him and wouldn't let him rest. So, he told them that. The two sisters spoke to each

[1]Two of the four kinship sections. Everyone belongs to either of the four sections. Purungu, Panaka, Karimarra and Milangha. These are structured according to specific social rules and regulate relationships within society, including who can marry whom

[2]A mother in law relationship; you are not allowed to face or approach a person who is tua to you

other, "We better let him come and sleep alongside the fire." Yeah, so alright, he came. He was getting a bit happy about that. He lay there for a while until he jumped up like a bullet out of a gun.

"The ants are getting me here too, everywhere here!" "Oh?" So the two sisters put their heads together to have a bit of a yarn. "Funny thing, he's on that side of the fire and we're on this side and the ants are on that side. We'll put him in between us." Right, they told him to lie in between them. Oh, he was happy as Larry. There was no ants there. So they slept there that night.

The next morning, they felt a bit hungry. In those days all the animals, especially birds, emus, turkeys — and snakes too — they had their eyes but they couldn't open them. They couldn't see, they could only smell. They had scum over their eyes like the newborn chicken or any puppy. The eyes are not open. So Pidadepina walked over to the pool to get some mandu, that's meat. He walked over to the pool at about sunrise, when all the birds, animals come in to water. He had a bit of a stick and knocked them on the head. It was easy since they couldn't see. He killed about a dozen or more.

While he was doing that, they sung out to him, "Pidadepina, Pidadepina, talangayanguna? Talanga-yanguna?" That meant, "Pidadepina, Pidadepina, where are you gone? Where are you gone?"

And he answered them, "Hu!"

So alright, they only wanted to know where he was. So they took off. They went across the Oakover River from Nilguna to these Two Sisters hills, Wilbagariganya.

When he came back with all these birds and that, some dead and some not, you know, half stunned, he looked around but couldn't see the two sisters. He had to put it all down and sing out to them for them to come and pick it up. He sung out. He said, "Two sisters, where are you gone?

Where are you gone?" No answer. He didn't know what to do. He took a circle around, cutting their tracks to see which way they went.

"Oh, they went this way."

He followed them a bit. He still had this meat left there, so he ran back. Pidadepina got hold of the oldest bird who was half dead, but still a little bit of life kicked in him, was left in him. He got hold of his bottom, turned him upside down and blew in his backside and his eyes opened up. Not only that one, but it opened the eyes of the whole lot up. They flew away and they could all see ever since.

He followed them right to this spot, these pyramid hills. He looked up and seen them. One had a firestick, which they always carried. They had very long hair, right down over their ankles. One said, "I'll lower my kurlkura down, grab it and I'll pull you up."

Right, he grabbed the hair, kurlkura. Oh, she pulled right up, very near up to the top. Then this other one said, "Well, you got the firestick." She burnt that hair alongside of his hands and let him drop down the bottom again and killed him.

That's Pidadepina. They killed him that way. That's the end of that story. The two hills are there and white people call them Two Sisters. The Aboriginal name for them two hills is Wilbagariganya. That's the Two Sisters on the road to Woodie Woodie Manganese Mine.

They used to tell us when we were kids you know. We would be sitting around the fire and the old people used to tell us all these sorta stories, all sorts. I forget a lot of them, the names and things you know.

There was a Dutchman. He found some gold way out at Martins, that's further east. It was difficult for him to cart the haul into the battery. It was cheaper for him to hire the battery, take it out to Martins and work the mine. They call it the Golden Granite. Well, he got a thousand ounces out of it, a thousand ounces out of somewhere around about five tonne. The only transport this Dutchman had was himself. He used to carry the parts of the battery across about five or six miles. He might make two trips a day. He'd carry a can and other boxes.

Old Mick Doherty and others shifted the battery out to Eastern Creek. Then they started there and found some good gold out at Elsie Mine. So they picked up this battery, they had bullock wagons then, and they put it out there and done a lot of work there with it at the Elsie Mine. When they finished out there, they took it back to Eastern Creek and it's still there. The battery's still there. There was no government help those days.

The gold was only worth two pound fourteen an ounce. The prospectors got together. They got a ten head battery, put it up. There was Mick Doherty and Tom Masterson and others. They found a big show up on top of a hill, what they call Doherty's Reward. There was Doherty's Reward, The Harp, and Morning Star. Doherty's Reward is still good if anyone can work it.

There's a dead man here

Childhood in Marble Bar and Port Hedland

Later, old Mick Doherty decided to take up a station, that's Meentheena. That's where my Aunty Dinah went. Mick started that with Harry Jenkins and Maurice McKenna. On Meentheena Station, Aunty Dinah got mixed up with Mick Doherty and she had two children by him, Clancy and Jack. Maurice McKenna got into trouble over cross-branding cattle, Warrawagine cattle. He had to do two years behind bars and at that time they let the station go, you know, back to the government.

My Aunty Dinah came back from Meentheena to work for the Sergeant, Strapp, in Marble Bar. So Sergeant Strapp* came out in a buggy and pair, him and a postmaster called Frank Williams. They picked me up and they took me. See, I was bitten by a dog, so they took me to the hospital. Doctor Triado was the doctor there at the time. I was with Sergeant Strapp and his family for three years. They took me in, the

---

*Strapp was actually a Corporal, a rank above Constable discontinued by 1917

Sergeant and his wife. They had two boys, about my size. They took care of me and they looked after me.

In 1910, I saw Halley's Comet. But that was funny that, no one never knew anything. No wireless, no anything, only newspapers. They used to get a newspaper, I think about once every two months or something, whenever the mail coach went through. But this time, we were all down the recreation ground, a lot of kids playing there. It was a dark night and this night some of them went to sleep quick, lay anywhere, you know what kids are like. Just as I was going to sleep, I looked up east, "Oh daylight, hey come on you fellas, we got to go home now, it's daylight."

In the meantime, there's a blackfella there called Black Billy Maher. He played a trick on us. He didn't know anything about this Halley's Comet. He got a dead man's skull from somewhere and he put it by the road that went over the top of this hill. Anyhow, I said, "Come on, we better go now, go home now." So we started to walk up. When we got up near, it was getting brighter, the Halley's Comet. But it wasn't quite far up then, just very light, you know, clear.

We looked behind, "Oh, there's dead man here, devil-devil." We turned around and went back and covered up in the blanket with our old aunty, Aunty Dinah. We watched this thing coming. "Oh well, this is the end of the world," we thought. Everybody thought, cause we had no communication up anywhere. It was very pretty, it was like a kite, you know. That's what shape it looked, a very long tail and it was all colours. It didn't last very long, it went straight west, went other side. That was 1910. So, I've seen two Halley's Comets. That one and one in 1985 when the teachers took me out on the middle of the road on the bitumen there. I must be one of the few people to have seen the comet twice.

The government building in Marble Bar was built by a German man. His name was Gerhard.[*] It's a fine building,

---

[*]The name of the contractor was Charles Darley and the contract price £7949.11.2. It took ten months to build

made out of stones. There was no cement those days. He used to make his own lime, burn it. You'd see his pits up there everywhere. I don't know how long it took him to build it, but it's a very long building. There's the post office, the court — the court house — clerk of courts, the police office and police quarters. See, it was a very big job. Well, that poor old fella, he finished up in a bad way.

Him and Warden Kelly went out in a buggy and pair, turkey shooting one afternoon. When they got to the place where they seen the turkeys, that was at a place called Stray Shot. Warden Kelly said to old Gerhard, "You hang onto the reins while I go and shoot this turkey." So Gerhard did, but when old Kelly fired the shot at the turkey, these horses jumped and snatched the reins out of Gerhard's hands. He was pulled too, and the leg of his pants got caught up in a swingle bar. Gerhard got caught up in that and was dragged all the way to the town on the gravel road. He had big blisters. He was almost dead when he got there.

They took him up to the hospital. Well, us mob of kids running around there, pulled the buggy up. We didn't know there was somebody underneath it. Anyhow, Billy Maher come along and stopped the horses. They took Gerhard up to the hospital. He used to have a very long beard, but that was all gone. He only lived about eight minutes and he was dead. That was old Gerhard. He had a little business of his own too. He was a baker. He'd bake the bread. He was a good old fella.

Warden Kelly, he was alright. Because the buggy went off, he come behind carrying this turkey. He was alright, but he wasn't alright when he found out that this other fella got killed though, the poor chap. They had the funeral the next day. There was no such thing as a post mortem in those days. You could bury a person anywhere as long as he was dead. Just wrap him up in his blankets.

One day Warden Kelly, the same man who used to go out with old Gerhard until the accident, went out on his own.

When he got back to Marble Bar pub, he pulled up in front of the pub to go in and have a few drinks, when he seen this old fella laying outside drunk. It was wintertime. He woke this old fella up, "Come on." He put him in the buckboard, covered him over with blankets and took him home. He didn't say anything to anyone. All he did was unharness the horses out of the buckboard, take them to the stables and feed them. This old fella was still laying covered up in the blankets.

That night, about midnight, a Chinaman died not far from where that buggy was, maybe three or four hundred yards away. Everybody sung out, "Oh, Chinaman died!"

"Oh, yeah?"

So they picked him up, "We'll take him to the Warden's buggy and put him in there."

By that time, this other old fella had woken up and walked away. They put this dead Chinaman in his place and covered him up with the same blankets.

In the morning, somebody walked up and told the Warden. "Warden, where Chinaman bin die last night?"

"Yeah? Oh, I better go and wake this other fella up. I picked him up in the pub yesterday. He was drunk."

It was daylight. When he came to wake him up, he saw a blooming Chinaman in there dead! The whiteman had gone. These other people didn't know anything about this other bloke. They'd just put the Chinaman in there and covered him up with the same blankets. Yeah well, that was a story a long time ago. A whitefella turns into a Chinaman, dead! That happened around about 1912.

Every station and every hotel in the Pilbara employed either Chinamen, Malays or Japanese cooks, no white cooks, they were too expensive. At the Esplanade, there was two Chinese cooks, one was the cook and the other one was an offsider, like that all the time. At the stations it was the same. They all had coloured cooks, no white cooks.

There was no school at Marble Bar at that time, but there were two hotels, the Ironclad and the Marble Bar Hotel. The Marble Bar Hotel was owned by Andy Elliot and the Ironclad was owned by Billy Maher. He owned a store as well. There was a fruit shop there too. Old Tom Matthews, he was some sorta Greek, old Tom, he owned the shop. If there was a little bit of dirty patch on an apple or whatever it was, he'd give it a lick and wipe it. Then he'd hand it over, "Here you are," and you'd give him a penny for it.

After that I was sent out to work, not hard work, looking after cows and things like that, you know. I went out to Stewart's Garden, an orchard and dairy farm in Marble Bar, on the bank of the Coongan River. There was me and Black Billy Maher and we were chasing each other. Aboriginals call that place Mikanna. They had milking cows there and everything like that. I used to cart the milk in every morning into Marble Bar town in a horse and sulky. I used to go with them and deliver the milk around, milkman they call them. I stayed with them for a while.

We came down to Port Hedland then in 1911, that's when I seen the first ships, the *Bullara* and the *Koombana*. In 1912, the *Koombana* went down, that was on the twenty-fourth of March. The strong winds and the heavy rain washed everything away; garden, house and everything at that place on the bank of the Coongan River. So, they couldn't keep me any longer.

They sent me to the Hedditch's family, Tom Hedditch, right in town. He had the pub then, the Esplanade Hotel. He was running the place. Before he was a sorta Road Board secretary there in Marble Bar. I used to chase cows for him while I was little, you know. I was with him for a while. He had two daughters. They were about my age. Our mistress, Katie O'Neil, used to look after us kids whenever we went to Hedditch. She was looking after us, she might have been teaching some of the others, other two girls. Two girls was Micky and Kathleen Hedditch, two sisters my age. We only seen her a couple of years ago at Marble Bar and Port Hedland. Katie O'Neil — after she got married to a postmaster, Bill McGovern, at Nullagine. She might have taught them, not me though.

Tom Hedditch had a station down here at Gorge Creek with George Arthur. He had a share in it, bought a share in it. In 1913, we came to Gorge Creek with cattle from Limestone Station. I used to lead the pack horse with George McGregor, he was a half-caste chap, and Black Billy Maher. We had a mob of cattle for Tom Hedditch. Had about a hundred cattle, brought them down to Poodubullara. Poodubullara was a yard there.

We yarded them that night and one cow gave birth to a calf there. Next day we went to Coongan pub. We took the cow with us, but the calf was left there, somewhere there. When we camped at the Coongan, that cow went back to the calf and got the calf, the cow did, that night. Next morning, Black Billy Maher said, "That cow go back I think, he not here."

"Oh."

"I go track 'em up and follow 'em, find 'em."

So, he went back and found the cow and calf, wasn't far from the Twelve Mile Yard. So he picked the calf up and put it in front of the pommel of his saddle, and brought the calf and cow back to the mob. We waited there at the Coongan, me and George McGregor.

Everyday we had to carry the calf. We went from there to Pear Creek I think it was, yeah. We had a night there. The next day we got to Gorge Creek, that's where the cattle had to go. We stayed there, might be three or four days, and Tom Hedditch wanted six milking cows and their young calves brought to Port Hedland. That was in 1913. We stopped there, stayed at the Esplanade Hotel for a while. I don't know, might've been five months or something like that.

While we kids were mucking around there in Hedland, where the Shell house is, or might be a bit back towards town, straight down from the Lock Hospital,* straight across, I seen a woman's track, a kid and a couple of dogs' tracks on these rocks on the surface of this hobble iron. I don't know where it is now, I suppose it's all bulldozed but it might still be there. They might have preserved it, you know, put something around it. Those tracks were going towards the sea, might have been half a dozen footprints on these rocks. Pretty wide the rock. There were the dogs' and a child's prints. Well, we don't know what happened there. No one never knew anything about them, you know, only by the tracks. It must have been there before Port Hedland was started, only just the tracks. We never seen any human beings, anything like that, only just the tracks on the rocks.

On the sandhill by the beach in a hollow place, there was a Afghan. He lived with a white woman, I don't know if he was married, but they were together. Well that's Mahomet, he was here as an agent for his country, to arrange delivery of camels that came out. One night, that woman disappeared and she hadn't been seen since, but ten years later somebody said, "Oh I think she must be buried down there." He's a terrible jealous man, no-good fella. That was somewhere around 1910, quite a while back. They used to take the camels then out to Carlindie, a place they called Camel Pool. They were quarantined there for quite a while.

There was no good water here in those days. There were little wells in Port Hedland, but the water was brackish. You couldn't get nice water to drink. You had to drink this brackish water. There was a well just behind where the Commonwealth Bank is now. There was another well near the Pier Hotel. The best one was at Four Mile, the Four Mile Ridge, when you come over the bridge. That was a govern-

*A place where patients were confined for treatment of infectious diseases

ment well. That was the best water. They used to come up there with horses and carts, and fill up their tanks and cart it into town. Some women used the same water three times to wash their clothes. They couldn't afford to get clean water, like what I mean, it was too far to get it. A lot of families didn't have horses and carts and things. Eventually, they got water on the train. They had big tanks. It used to come up here from Poondina. People used to fill their tanks up from the train's water.

So I got a brainwash

The start of my working life: Gorge Creek

At the end of 1913, they sent me back to Gorge Creek. I was old enough to work a little bit then, you know. I was there with the horse boys. That was the time we come, start to build the place up. Oh, they were! I was only playing with horses and things like that. The bosses, or whoever they had working for them, they were working around Gorge Creek there, cutting pots and putting fences and sinking down wells and bores and things like that.

One day the boss, George Arthur, and his mate had to go to Marble Bar on the train. They left me at the camp where they were sinking a well and I had the dogs there, little puppies. Any rate, they were supposed to go up there that morning and be back in the evening, you know. Well, they did do that, but when the sun was just before sundown, I was still by myself with these dogs.

I was frightened, didn't know what devil-devil might come and pick me up. So I was playing with these puppies, "I'm gonna make my bed in between them," I thought. They started laying on top of me and all that sorta thing. At that time, while I'm organising these things with the puppies, the boss walks up. "You're not supposed to play with puppies or any dogs if you want them to do anything! You got to treat them as dogs!"

Anyhow, I was playing with them. Of course I was only little fella, and then I got a hiding for that, terrible hiding! "Never play with puppies, never lie them on your bed." They bring germs, disease and all that sorta thing, you know. Even cats, some cats, the cats those days, they used to go out hunting and find a snake and half kill it. They'd bring it in half dead and play with it, you know, the pussycats. They are very dangerous, they might bring a half dead Death Adder in. If that bites you, well you're gone! "Never allow them inside the house, these cats." All things like that. I had to learn. So I got a brainwash.

We had a lot of nanny goats, billy goats out there. We made two wheels with a crosscut saw. It had an axle, a wooden axle I think it was — not too sure now. We used a beer case for a cart and put this billy goat on it. The billy goat used to pull the cart. I'd have the reins and be driving around. That's the only one thing I had to play with. Oh, you'd get a doll like, but very very seldom. They were all made out of clay. There were no plastic ones, that was unheard of, plastic. They were hard clay.

My stepfather, Sandy McPhee, found out where I was. Then in 1914, the war broke out and a big mob joined up to go to war. Anyway, he asked could he pick me up and take me to Port Hedland to see him off. My boss George Arthur said, "Yeah, you can take him." There was no carriages, just open trucks. He picked me up in Gorge Creek and brought me to Port Hedland to see him off. So, we stayed at the Esplanade Hotel again. We were waiting for the ship called *Bambra*, that's the ship they went on.

Oh, there was, could've been four or five hundred people like, soldiers, you know. They got on the *Bambra,* went to Fremantle and they were sent out to Blackboy Hill in Perth. They weren't there too long before they caught the boat to go overseas to Gallipoli. That was in 1915. My father and all his comrades, I don't know who they were, a lot of them.

It was just a slaughterhouse there and a lot of them got wounded and so on. They were sent back to London for treatment and when they finished, when they got alright, well, my father and three or four others — they were sent to Palestine, amongst the horses and camels and that was the end of him. That's where he died.

I was back at Gorge Creek then, but my father's brother was here, my uncle Billy McPhee. Well, he used to get all the messages and letters from them. He was telling me the story about what happened over there. My father's name was Sandy McPhee, some called him Alec — well, that stands for Sandy.

Sandy, Rory, Jimmy and Billy McPhee, they're all brothers, four of them. They split up here at De Grey. Billy, he stayed there all his life and Jim went north to the Northern Territory, never come back. Rory and Sandy, they went prospecting and they found a patch of gold between Lalla Rookh Goldmine and Lalla Rookh Station. I don't know what year that was. They call that McPhee's Patch.

They stayed there and it wasn't good enough. The gold those days was only worth two pound fourteen an ounce. There was two of them and a blackfella, so they headed for Moolyella. Tin was plentiful those days at Moolyella, you can pick it up just like that, anywhere and everywhere around Moolyella. That's out from Marble Bar, sixteen miles out from Marble Bar.

When they were on their way up, they camped at a place, a creek on the Talga River. The horses went up this little creek and in the morning the blackfella went to get the horses, he found a nugget, nugget of gold. He picked that up, took it back to the old man and his brother Rory. So, they worked there for a little while and got all the easy stuff, you know. That's Talga Mine, they call it now.

It wasn't good enough. They thought they'd do better on tin. You see, it was easy got, plentiful. That's at Moolyella. So they went to Moolyella and I don't know what year that was, could be the time I was born, might have been a bit before. I can't tell you the day, year or anything about that.

So, they heard, or some other people told them, they'd do better off on gold, west of Marble Bar, Paddy's Market and some of those other places, McLeod's Reward. So he found that place, but it was in quartz. It had to be crushed by a battery, there was no batteries around those days, not there.

You see, the nearest battery was seventy miles at Marble Bar. Well, they had to cart that, they had no vehicle of any kind. All they had was pack horses. So, they'd give it up. They went back to the tin again, they were better off on tin.

That was the time he picked me up, Sandy adopted me and my mother. Then they went and done — someone told them two they might do good at Sharks Gully. They found a lump of gold there, oh monster, west of Marble Bar, about twenty-six miles, Sharks Gully.

From there, when they worked, everything got hard and that, you know, for them, so they went to Nullagine and they found a patch there, McPhee's Patch. So they got a battery, I don't know who from, might be from Mick Doherty. I think it was a little three head battery.

They stayed there and they threw it up and they went back to Moolyella, went back on the tin. It's much easier to get the tin, the tin was only two and six a pound that time. They done alright you know, they could make a living out of it, but not with gold. Gold was alright if they could get it in big lumps all the time and I suppose they drank a bit too, I don't know. But they found McPhee's Patch, that's at Lalla Rookh.

Talga workings, twenty two miles this side of Marble Bar, they found a goldmine — wasn't a goldmine then — and Sharks Gully, they found that, and they found near Edies Well, they found that one. They found four, five shows.

That's what different ones was telling me, old people, white people. I found that just talking about it, but full history of them otherwise, I don't know because I was too young. You must remember, I was nine years old, what would I know about it? When he went away in 1914.

Rory, he stayed, he was too old or there was something wrong with him, but I know he was too old to go to the war. Sandy was the only one and Billy was too young and the other fella, Jim, he was — I don't know how old he was. I think he was the eldest one, he never came back.

So that's the story of him, Sandy. I can't tell you anymore about that, about him otherwise. But I know they only had pack horses, they didn't have any carts or wagons or drays or anything like that to do anything good.

They were both single. They camped at Murphy's Gap at Moolyella. They had one camp at Murphy's Gap and they had another camp at King Tin Creek, where they were getting tin you know, dry-blowing and all that sorta thing, and that's where he went from. That's where he joined up from.

Anything else, I can't tell you because I don't know. I was too young. He looked after me and mum. Picked mum up and took me and mum to his camp where he was tin working you know, Murphy's Gap, east twenty-one miles out of Marble Bar. But I can't tell you anymore about that, about anything else. Some say this and some say that, but I know this story from different ones, what I'm just telling you. This is a true story about him and his brother, Rory McPhee. I knew him pretty well, you know. I used to see him often.

Jimmy didn't want to stay and Rory and Sandy, stepfather, went prospecting.

There is this story I'm going to tell you about. Old Jack Christie, he had a bullock team. He was coming down this way, empty. I was only a little fella, I think it must've been in 1916. We saw the wagon on the road as we were going home in the spring cart. The boss said, "Oh, the team is up here, bullocks are all feeding now." Big Condamine bells on them. When we got there, old Billy Lennard was laying up against the pony wheel. He must have lit a fire after he let the camels and bullocks go and put his billy on the fire. When we come along at about five o'clock, I suppose, the sun was pretty low and the boss sung out, "G'day." He knew the fella. "G'day Billy, how are you? Were you going to sleep there?" No answer. So the boss got off to start waking him up. He was dead!

The nearest telephone was twelve miles away from there. We had to turn around and go back to the telephone and notify the Marble Bar police. We travelled all night in the spring cart back to Gorge Creek Homestead. The police came out next day or might've been two or three days later. They just scratched a bit of a hole there by the road and rolled him into it. The grave is still there, quite clear. Old Billy Lennard, I knew him a little bit, but my boss knew him properly. He was a bullock teamster.

I'll tell you some Aboriginal custom, but I can only give you bits and pieces here and there.

One woman over there has got a young boy, another woman over here has got a young girl. Well, they'd be cousins, them two mothers. This boy, he'd be son-in-law of this other one. So this other one gives this boy her daughter as a sorta gift, see. Get them sorta married. That was the legal way of getting wives. Nobody could touch this woman. Tua means you can't go near her. You can talk to her from a distance of a few feet away but not closer. They call that tua, some call them madugu. The boy and the girl will be legally married.

Of course, they can leave each other and that was always happening too. You wasn't allowed to have a woman unless somebody give them to you. They'd either kill you or spear you, do something to harm you.

Yeah marriage! Say now you want to break the law. Say, there's a girl there, I'd like to have her — but I'm not, in ordinary terms, allowed to. But they know that I want her and she wants me, but we're not allowed to get together. There's one way to do that. They get the boy, they get the girl and they get them to pull one another's hair. Like that. They are right then. They can get married after that. They can have each other then. That tribal law is broken, finished. They can get married. It's hard to believe, but that's how it is.

Food, eating snakes, carpet snake, you can eat them. I tried one once, but I couldn't eat it, awful taste. That's buliyuriya you know, black carpet snake. He's got a black head. Funny taste, he's all fat, all the way from his tail to his head, like a rope. Fat, oh terrible fat!

Kangaroo meat. See, the old people were very strict. I'm talking about way back. If you got a kangaroo, the kangaroo, it's got to be given to you by one of the Heads[1] to eat. You just couldn't go up and grab a bit of meat! Oh no, that's out of the question altogether!

If anybody dies, say some of the relations, well they go what they call tadi.[2] You're not allowed to eat beef or mutton. You can eat any bush meat bar that. They put you on that diet until such time as the Heads decide your mourning is finished. Usually about five years. That never happened to me, but we had a fella with us. We were out mustering and one fella said to me, "This fella never ate any meat!"

"No? Well, we can't feed him on damper all the time. We'll have to make him eat the meat." Well, what you do, what they did, you get a piece of meat and sneak up behind him. See, he might be sitting there and they get this meat and

---

[1]Elders   [2]Special state involving taboos

rub it all over his face and he's finished. He has a good cry and all the rest of it like that and he's allowed to eat meat again. The tadi is finished. That's how it goes. But I've never had that happen to me, they never done that to me — tadi business.

We used to go out to Condon, crabbing. Condon is on De Grey. It's on the coast. The old bridge is still there, the stones and things like that. On the other side of that creek, Condon Creek, when you go around you come to a black rock and when the tide is up, you'll be surrounded with sea water. Black Rock that's called. Oh, terrible place for big rock cod. Oh, big ones! They caught one there, they couldn't lift it. They had to get a Jeep, ropes and pull it away before the water came. They had to go down so they could lift the rock cod up. It took two men. You often catch big rock cods there. You can always hear them if you don't catch them. You can get rock lobsters there and there are a lot of oysters growing there. Good place for fishing, good camping ground. I been there many of times with my family.

A chap by the name of Tiffany was one in charge out there and the post office was back this way, half way up the sandhill. An oleander tree is growing there. It is a Commonwealth Government post office. All the bullockies and teamsters, some had horse wagons, camels. They were all drunkards these people. Whisky drinkers, rum. Some of them were called "rum tasters," that was Ned Roche.

But anyway, we came up for a race meeting, this special time, and I think there was about ten horses. They had a racecourse, rough one, you know? No graders those days, all pick and shovel, just out on the clear ground there where the post office is. In a race, their horses had to gallop three miles, a three mile course. Oh well, this time I was told about this fella by old Jack Walker, who was there when it happened.

One fella, he got cunning. He trotted his horse around, trotted it, sometimes fast walking, and in the last lap he dug his spurs into the horse's ribs and away he went. He won the race because his horse was fresh, the other ones were knocked up because they were galloping all the time!

At the foreshore near the goods sheds, the pearling luggers came in and delivered these pearls in great big bags for this fella, Banjo his name. I don't know what his other name was. Then he'd send them away, these pearls. I don't know who owned the pearling luggers. There were a lot of Malays and, you know, all colours they were, Singhalese and Koepanger. I think there were about a dozen in a crew. A couple of divers and then there's the skipper. There might have been two of those. The shell opener, a couple of them, then there's the cook. Ah, there must have been about ten or twelve of these fellas. They used to go out about six weeks at a time and they'd come in and unload and get their food, water and stuff. They were all along the beach up here, on the Eighty Mile Beach. Little wells with fresh water and these pearling luggers knew where they were. Of course — going out once — they'd know them all.

They had canvas bags that'd be about two feet long, water bags, they'd carry them over to the well. The well might be about half a mile off the beach. They'd fill these bags up and carry them back to their lugger. They might make two or three trips like that, enough to last them for a month or six weeks.

I remember when I was a boy around 1914-15, an old fella, he was a shearer, very short-sighted. Well, there were no machines those days. He had two horses, one was a pack horse. At this side of Marble Bar, there was a hotel, Coongan Pub. This old chap was called Bluey Adams. Well, he'd come in there with a two bob in his pocket and he let his horses go.

I was there at the time he got stuck into the grog. He'd drink that much, he'd lay anywhere and everywhere, dirty, filthy, old Bluey. When he ran out of cash, he'd sell one of his horses to get a few more bob. He'd keep going like that and he'd sell his riding gear, that's the bridle and saddle. When he drank that up, he'd sell the pack horse and he'd drink all that money, and the packs and the pack saddles — clean them, clean them all up. There was quite a few of those old chaps.

When the First World War ended in 1918, you could see a lot of people walking along carrying their swags. They couldn't get a job. They'd go around asking people if they could get a bit of tea and sugar or a bit of bread, something to eat. Oh, you'd see that day after day. It was terrible. That's how it was with the white Australian people, but the Europeans and Asians never carried swags. All the Italians, Germans and Chinamans were very cunning with their money, with whatever money they did have. It's only the dinky-di Australian, he was starving. The Sandgropers, the West Australians and of course the South Australians, the Crow Eaters.

Around that time, I used to run away sometimes to Warralong, they'd fetch me back. There was no such thing as getting away because you had the policeman after you. Of course, they couldn't do nothing, just pick you up and take you back, especially a kid, you know.

Chasing Brumby horses

Droving, working as a station hand

In 1918 I met Harry Farber, who had been breaking in horses at Warralong. He asked me would I like to go with him. I said, "You would have to see the boss." So we run out there in a old T-model Ford to where George Arthur was putting down a bore.

A few days later, Harry Farber picked me up and took me north droving, I was big then, you know, working. Well, I was thirteen by that time. We went up as far as Rollah Downs Station, not far from La Grange Bay. We had three hundred head of cattle, it could've been a few more. First we had to take the cattle to La Grange Bay dip because of the ticks, the fever and anything like that. I think the person who ran the dip was named Hamilton. We dipped all the cattle and then we had to hold them around until the next day. We dipped them again because the ticks was very very bad, some of them was as big as a thumbnail, very big. When we finished dipping them, we lost seventy head, I think. Well, they died from what they called Red Water. They got Red Water, I don't know what that means.*

We left there and came through Frazier Downs Station, and from there to a place called Black Tank. That was on Calanjadie Station. We watered the cattle there and went to McPhee's Well. The water was very very shallow; we must've watered about a hundred head. You bale it out dry, you know. They used to send me down — I was only a kid — with a tin to fill the bucket up.

When we left there, we went to a place called One Tree Well. Then we went from there to Marlambool Well. We watered the cattle there. Then we went to Nambeet Well and we watered them there. Then from there, we came to Naljee and from there to Wallal post office. Those days there was a post office at Wallal. There was a cattle dip there too. We dipped them there three times. Then we went from there to a place called Yinadong and from there to Warangol. We stayed there two days watering them and all that sort of thing.

We had to cross the desert — no water. It took us three days to go across. There was water for us, we had waterbags and the horses, the horse saddler used to bring the horses back and take our horses to water them. We were three days on that. We travelled day and night. We came to a place called Rabbit Well. We didn't water the cattle there because there wasn't enough water, only for the horses. The next day, we came to a big claypan on Yarrie Station. Oh, it was a great big thing. Then we went from this claypan to Quartz, a big pool on the Oakover River. We followed this river up to Pindah post office.

There was a big pool there. That's on Warrawagine Station. Then we went from there to a big pool on the river called Wanggugabunha. Then we went from there to Chukuwalyee, a big pool there, no shortages of water. Then

*A cattle disease of the blood caused by parasite Babesia, carried by tick as vector

we went from there to a windmill called the Little River, Kurlukurluwayinha, and we camped at the place where Mrs Hodgson had the baby at Lambing Creek, or Young Hodgson's Creek I think they call it now.

We went to Braeside, plenty of water, and from there we went to Midgengadge Pool, then to the next one to Carawine, a big pool there. That's the gorge and from there to Tooma, a big pool there, never goes dry. From there to Running Waters, and from Running Waters to Eel Pool on the Davis River. Then to Pulpulgara and Skull Springs, plenty of water. Then from there we went to Horses Creek, then from there to Billin Ballin, plenty of water.

The next day, we went to Shag Pool. From Shag Pool, we had no water until we got to Moolna Rockhole. Then from there we went to Kullawarri Windmill and from there we went to Seventeen Mile Windmill and tank. The next water was Eight Mile Windmill, that's on Roy Hill, and from there we went to a big pool, Meecardagunna, Migaraganha. Then, the next water was Engine Well on Ethel Creek Station. From there we went to Jimblebar Pool and the next water was a government well called Murramunda. From Murramunda to another government well, Spinifex Well, very deep. The next government well is on the Savory Creek that runs out to the desert. There is a dead end to that creek out there, at a place called Disappointment.

From there to Mundiwindi, another government well there. Then to well Number Nine.[1] The next well was Number Eight and Number Seven Well. Then Number Six Well and Number Five Government Well[2] and the next water is Saddlegunna. We went from there to Bore Well, then to Jiboongunna Pool and to a place called Rabbit Well. From there to Three Rivers Station, there's a pool of water there, part of the Gascoyne River. There's a homestead beside it, Three Rivers Station. Then the next water we got was Beasley's Big Claypan and then another government well they call Mox Well. From there we went to Narracoota and

1Actually Well 39   2Actually Well 35

then to Ruby Well, a government well. Then to Thirty-Two Mile government well, they call that Karalundi today. There's a mission not far from there with gardens and things.

From there we went to Munarra Government Well and then to a little pool with plenty of water for cattle, a place called Banjo Pool. From Banjo Pool to the Eleven Mile Government Well and then into the trucking yards in Meekatharra. That was the end of our journey. We trucked all the cattle there and we split up. Harry Farber, he went to Perth.

I worked on Yarlarweelor for a while for Jack Matthews. Well, we did all stock work. Riding horses, looking for cattle, pinching cattle from different ones. Well, they were pinching them, I was only a lad looking after the horses and tuckerbox. They were pinching the cattle from other people and putting their brand on them. That's what you call cattle-duffing. You might find a cow with a calf with no brand on it. They'd grab the calf and put their brand on it. We went through Prairie Downs, Turee Creek, Mt Vernon, Mulgul, Milgun, Woodlands, Yarlarweelor, Mt Padbury, Mt Seabrook, all through there. That was all just wild country, open country with a lot of stock, cattle. There was no such thing as fences.

They sent me out to Donkey Jones on the road to Mooloogool, Diamond Well Station and Lake Way. Lake Way, Wiluna that is. They used to call that Lake Way in the early days, Lake Naberoo not far from the goldmine. They changed the name to Wiluna when the railway started going through there, somewhere around about 1929. Mooloogool and Diamond Well Stations were owned by Pattersons those days. Their homestead was at Wongawol. Jimmy Jones owned — Donkey Jones, everyone called him Donkey Jones because he had a lot of donkeys, no sheep, no cattle. I was looking after the donkeys there. As long as they have plenty of water, donkeys don't take much looking after, so Jimmy used to go and do a lot of work for others. One day he took me to Windy Springs where we done a bit of work for old Bill Snell. He had cattle there. Bill Snell owned a few places out there, Bald Hill and Eladgie, that was part of his too. That's where the Canning Stock road comes in from Billiluna. After that we went back home, back to Donkey Jones.

There was two brothers, George Evans and Johnny Evans. Well, George Evans come to me one night at about eight o'clock. He said, "What about coming out to Murchison Downs, Jack? I want to pick up some shearers out there." He said, "It'd be a bit rainy, the road is awful."
I said, "Okay." So way we went out, opening gates. There was no run-throughs those days. You had to open every gate, sheep country. Anyway, we got out there at about breakfast time, we had breakfast at Murchison Downs and they packed up the old Dodge car and trailer; the shearers, me and Johnny, he was the driver of course. He was driving for Campbell & Co.
  So anyway, when we got along the road a bit on the way into town, one tyre blew off the wheel. We couldn't find it. It was too dark. So one shearer said, "Well, while we're walking around here and can't find it, I'll walk into town and get someone to come out." So George Evans said, "Right, that's a good idea. Well, if you go in, ask for Prince, Prince Gibson. He knows the road out here. Tell him to bring out a tyre." Anyway, he came back with it. So we put that wheel on and took it to the shearers into town. I was hanging around there, holidaying sorta business while I was supposed to be working for Jimmy Jones out at Twelve Mile, twelve miles out from Meekatharra.

It was 1920 and Harry Farber wanted me back. We went chasing brumbies at Eladgie Springs, Bridal Face, around Bald Hill and all that country out at Lake Naberoo, a place called Collarah. That's the name of the station out there and Yandil out near Wiluna. Yandil was owned by Henry Sprigg. Collarah was owned by Harry Greene. We were chasing brumby horses out at Mt Yagahong on Hillview Station near Gabanintha. There's a pub there, the Gabanintha Hotel. We were at Yarrabubba Station for quite a while, Ned and Alec Meehan's Station that was. Brumbies are very hard to get hold of, to catch you know, wild. After that, we went to gather up all our donkeys, mules and horses in Meekatharra. They're out in the commonage there, and we started off north droving again.

There was this fella. They called him Dingo Dann. He used to catch wild dingoes. He'd kill them, poison them, anything like that. He never really worked for anybody. He'd get a few dingo scalps. I think they're only two pound ten a scalp. He might get nine or ten of those. Well, that'll keep him goin' for twelve months.

He'd go to Balfour Downs Station. He'd start off there. They'd fill his tucker bag up as much as he could carry. He'd go down to the first water hole, lie there and eat most of that up. Then he'd go from there to Meentheena Station. The manager would say, "Hello Dann, how are you?"

"Oh," he said, "I'm pretty hungry. The blokes up at Balfour Downs wouldn't give me any tucker." But they'd given him that much he could hardly carry it!

So, the manager said, "Oh well, how are you off for tucker, for tea?"

"Oh, I got hardly anything!"

"Oh well, you better come over to the kitchen and have tea and breakfast there with us. I'll fill your bag up to carry on to Warrawagine."

"Yeah alright, that'll do."

So, he got that and went to a water melon patch. They used to grow wild there on the rivers. There might be forty, fifty water melons there. Well, he'd make a camp and stay there until he'd cleaned them all up. It might take him a week. People got sick of all the water melons, but he was in his glory! Oh, he was a funny man! He'd continue from there and get to Warrawagine. When he gets there, he'd talk to the manager. "Oh," he said, "I'm pretty hungry, I haven't had a feed for about two days"

"Oh, where did you come from?"

"Meentheena."

"Oh," he said, "What's wrong with the manager up there? Didn't he give you anything?"

"Oh, he's no good, he didn't give me anything."

"Well, I'll give you something to go on with. Which way are you gonna go?"

"Oh," he said, "I'll go up the Oakover to Balfour Downs again."

This went on for about two or three years like this. Anyhow, he'd given that job away and in 1921 we all went up droving to the Kimberley. Dingo Dann wasn't working with my lot, my team. He was working for Paddy Matthews, but we're all doing the same job sorta. We went up to Carnot Bay past Beagle Bay. The Carnot Bay Station didn't have enough cattle. We got some from Lombadina. Dingo Dann was the cook. While we were waiting for Paddy Matthews who got a mob of cattle from Beagle Bay, Dann and I went down the beach at Willie Creek. There was only him and me there, all the others went on to get the cattle. Anyhow, he said to me, "Jack, I'm gonna go down throw a line in the water at Willie Creek." I said, "Okay."

So he caught a big, oh a very big dugong. He said, "Well, that'll do us." We took him to the camp and he cooked it. I got a little piece out of that, not much because he gobbled it up as fast as he could. I don't know where he used to put it all. He was a pretty big man of course. We had a big fifteen inch camp oven, a drover's camp oven. He used to make dampers and brownies in it. A brownie'd be fifteen inches across, he'd give me a slice and then he'd cross his legs alongside of the brownie. He'd stop there until he almost got halfway through it. He'd clean the other half up too. Oh, he was a terrible man to eat!

I don't know what happened to him in the end. He was a terrible greedy man, terrible. Oh yeah, he could eat, he could eat no doubt about it! He could eat a leg of mutton for one meal. It's hard to believe. I think too much food killed him, that's what I think, when he got a bit old, you know. Well, he was pretty old when I seen him last in 1952 at Peak Hill.

We brought them cattle back to Roy Hill. It was 1922 when we got to Roy Hill. Then we left those cattle there and got another mob to Cue, Austin Downs Station, old John Patrick Meehan and sons. When we finished that trip, we went to Roy Hill, Hillside, Marble Bar and down the Coongan River to Mulyie and De Grey Station. We took five thousand wethers there, sheep.

The eclipse of the sun was on at Wallal then. People from all over the world came to that. They had things written up there weeks, months before that. It went dark for about an hour, couldn't see nothing — only stars. All the nationalities of the world came to there.

They were prepared for it. They had everything; telescopes and everything rigged up on concrete blocks and all that sorta thing — to see the eclipse of the sun. Well, we seen it, we were in the dark. We was up near Muccan at that time. That was in 1922. Well, that was the end of my droving trip. Harry Farber, the boss I had at the time, was a terrible man. He was German descent. He was the only German that I ever knew that was no good. They all said that, it's very funny. Most of the foreigners, people from Germany, Belgium or France was very good to Aboriginal people in this country. It was only the white dinky-di Australians that was no good to us. Whatever the trouble was there, I don't know. He'd treat you like a dog. We wasn't allowed to go to school or anything like that. We wasn't allowed to know anything. One fella said, one squatter, "Why don't you send him to school, Harry?"

"Oh," he said. "You never want to do that with a blackfella, he'd know too bloody much and he'd be telling you what to do. You want to keep them down as low as the bloody ground," he said. He was a very cruel boss, terrible cruel man he was. I used to cop a lot, all the hidings. I'd get all the blame. If someone else did the wrong thing, I'd get blamed for it. So I ran away and got away from him.

Out bush

You got your orders first thing in the morning

I went to Warralong Station and worked there, just a casual job for two, three weeks. Then I went from there to Bungalow Station, I was there for about one year. That's when I went through the Law, Aboriginal Law, everything about Aboriginal culture, that's Nyamal, that's the tribe. I had almost forgotten about all the Aboriginal business. So when I came back, I was able to talk and learn to talk tribe business and everything in the Aboriginal way with my aunty, Aunty Dinah. It didn't take me long to pick it all up again.

Out on Coojinarilna Creek, that's on Mulga Downs Station, a man got shot. Toby and Gunstock — Gunstock, his foot got hurt some time and when it healed up, it healed up just like the stock of a gun.

Well, Toby and Gunstock, they were the ones that was after old Dick's woman. That was the night they shot old Dick, but the bullet didn't go into his head. They had taken the lead out

I told him, "Jack McPhee."

At the foreshore near the goods sheds, the pearling luggers came in.

The creek in front of the Esplanade was running a banker. Cyclone 1939

I came down to Port Hedland...

In the finish, the front of the radiator was all cement

The gravestone reads:

DR. ED VINES
SPEARED
BY NATIVES
SEPT. 1899
†

Mrs Hodgson was going to have a baby. That's why Dr Vines was there

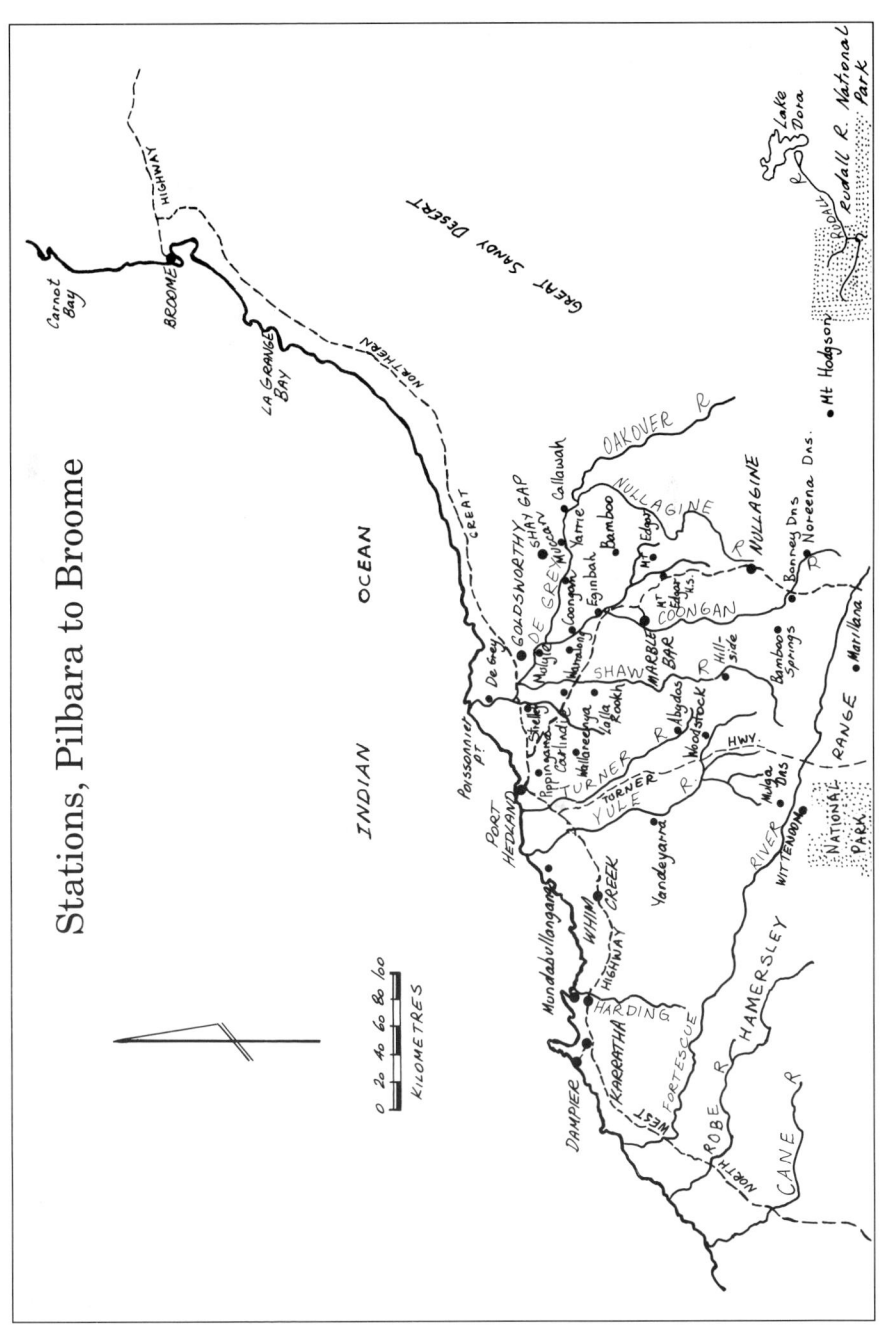

Stations, Pilbara to Broome

One fella had a camel team, they called him the White Khan

I had a few bob in the bank, so I bought a T-model Ford...

and away they went to the woman. They had a mob of dogs with them.

Come down mustering cattle and who should be coming along the road? Bill Dunnet, the boss of Mulga Downs. A dog come out of the cave in the rock on a bit of a hill and rushed up to Dunnet. He was on horseback. Dunnet had a look at him. He said, "That's not a dingo that fella, he's a tame dog." So he hunted the dog and the dog run back to old Dick in the cave. Dunnet followed him and sees this old blackfella in there.

"G'day old fella. What's the matter with you?"

He said, "Djulugu, somebody."

"Yeah, where? Didn't the bullet go in?"

"He shoot 'im there," old Dick said, pointing at his forehead.

"Yeah, well I can't see no hole there. See? Got burnt, you know, with the powder — must've been."

"Oh well. Can you walk?"

"Little bit," old Dick tell him. "Little bit."

"Oh, I'll go back to the camp, I'll get the truck and take you to Balfour Downs and get the policeman or welfare or somebody to come out and pick you up."

So he did that and they sent for old Dick but he wasn't harmed. No harm was done to him at all, only just the powder burnt his forehead. Toby and Gunstock went out in the desert somewhere. They never found them no more. Oh, they turned up later on, after six or seven months. They didn't come back there, but back to another station, Warrawagine, I think.

There was two jackaroos on a place, a black one and a white one. They're riding along together and the black one, he been there so long he didn't know how long! He said to the white one, I think his name was Billy, he said, "Billy, I'd like you to make my count up."

"Oh?" he said.

"When did you start, Jimmy?"

"Oh," Jimmy said. "I forget now, let me thinkum for a little while…Oh, I remember! I started…I know when I started, Une, Uly, August, Spletember, knock 'em down, no bloody wonder." That means June, July, August, September, October, November.

"Oh, righto, how much a week you gettin?"

"Oh," Jimmy said, "Thirty bob a week, thirty bob a week."

"Oh yeah, well you'll have so much. You been buying stuff at the store, I s'pose."

"Oh yeah, I buy some stuff. I don't know how much I got. Might be fifty pound, might be seventy pound, I don't know."

"Oh, I see. Aah, have you got a woman?"

"No, I'm a single fella, I got no woman."

"Oh? Oh well, you might have…I'll work this out tonight what pay you got. You'll have to get a bill from the storekeeper and see what you owe and bring this up and I'll work it out for you."

"Yeah, alright."

So he did that!

"Oh," Jimmy said, "I'm much rich fella now." He got fifty pound in cash to come to him. "I'm a rich fella now. I'll go for a pinkeye."

The white jackeroo, Billy, said, "What's pinkeye?"

"Oh well, you go walkabout, holiday."

"Oh yeah, oh well, you'll have plenty of money."

"Oh yeah, got plenty of money. Might buy some clothes and go chasing bungarras and things like that. Go corroboreeing."

"Oh," Billy said, "Oh well, when you going Jimmy?"

He said, "I think next week, the boss…I'll see the boss tomorrow. I want to go next week."

"How far you going?"

"Oh, not far. Not too far. The next station, around about, go corroboreeing and havin' plenty fun."

"Oh yeah."

"Then I come back, when I've had my pinkeye." Pinkeye means holiday in Aboriginal way. Jimmy and Billy, they were mainly at Mulyie and De Grey.

Backwards and forwards there, they used to shift them about, you know. If they're short handed at this place, they'd go and hire other fellas from the other station for a few weeks to break in horses and things like that. We'd do a little bit of everything — horse work, little bit of sheep work, little bit of cattle work and sometimes they get donkeys or camels. You go around the fences, boundary riding as they call it. You might go and help somebody else on other work, like sinking a well or putting up a fence or work in the sheep yards and things like that. You do a little bit of everything, especially while you're waiting for the big jobs to come along. You're all over the place and all you live on is bread and meat, damper and black tea and corned beef or corned mutton. That was your tucker, what you get when you go out in the bush.

It was very hard here, in the early days, very hard. Say from 1918 to about 1927-28, very hard for nearly anybody, even white people. The highly paid man, he'd be the manager, he'd get about five quid a week. The ordinary man, the jackaroo or the overseer, he'd get about two to three quid a week. Some only get thirty bob, like that. The money situation was very, very hard. But the things you bought, clothing and that, was cheap. In the stores, you'd get a pair of trousers for twenty-five bob and shirt for about twelve and six, might be six bob, all depends on the quality. You might do that twice a year. You'd get no hand-outs.

Squatters were very, very hard those days. All the money they got for their cattle, wool or sheep, they send away and buy a big flash house in Perth, Sydney, Melbourne or Adelaide. There was not too much put back on the people that was working on the place, not much improvement made on the place. They'd work it that way, you know, and get rich, go for a trip to England or wherever they want to go. Their wives would stop away, because it was too hard up here and hot. Wintertimes they'd usually come up, only for about five or six weeks, then they go back home again to their big mansions in the city.

The squatter he stops up here, most of the time. He might go away for a week or a fortnight and he'd be back again. We might start well sinking to get water. Put up windmills, tanks or troughs around the mill, put a bit of a yard around the well, all that sorta thing.

Well, that's the routine of work. You had to do a little bit of everything, you know, mix it all up. There might be two men out here, three men out there and a mob of men out on a big job or something like that. You had to learn all those things, anything at all, whatever comes.

You got your orders first thing in the morning, straight after breakfast. The manager or the overseer comes out and tells you what to do for the day. Most of the times, there'll be a cook cooking dampers, meat or brownies or something like that. There's nothing better than brownies. There were no sweets of any other kind and there'd be just ordinary plain meat and damper. You could get a bit of sour bread and sour tea when you're back at the homestead.

There'd always be a kerosene tin at the front of the kitchen door and all the teapots were emptied into this square, four gallon kerosene tin. Well, at the end of the week, the cook puts it on the stove and puts more water in it if it needs it. That's how you got your tea.

Well, milk, they had milk but you very seldom ever get that. They had cows, milking cows. You might get a bit of that, but it'd be from the day before or the day before that. You didn't get any fresh milk, that goes to the heads. You got the old stuff, might be a little sour, gone all mouldy, you know, curdly.

When shearing time comes, they might send a couple of blokes or one bloke to the other shearing people, to the next station, next-door to pick out their sheep and take them back to their own place. You'd have a rattle with different coloured tags in your pocket. You'd look at the earmark of the sheep and pull out a tag and put it on the sheep, sometimes it's red or sometimes blue. The blue would be for the station you work on and the red for say, the next-door.

The sheep are easy to pick out then, when they're going through the race,* when they're drafting them off. There'd be a lot of dust, so much you can't see yourself in the sheep yard or cattle yard. Dust all the time. Some people get sickness out of it. They get their lungs dusted and can't breathe. They have to go to hospital, that's if the manager says, "Yeah, send him to hospital."

Sometimes he'll say, "Oh he's alright, leave him go, but if he gets any worse and is still alive, well, take him in." It was very, very hard, things was very tough. You got good managers and bad ones. If you got a good manager, he'll take you in straight away. Other managers will say, "I'll take him in next week, he might be a bit worse, that's if he is still alive, I'll take him in and if he's not, if he's dead we'll dig a hole and bury him."

Those days, there was no such thing as notifying the police or doctor or anything like that. There'd be no post-mortem. If anybody died suddenly, they used to dig a hole, a grave, roll him up in his blankets or something, put him in and cover him up. It was very hard.

An old white chap, they called him Dobson of Australia, he used to carry his swag up and down wherever he went. Well, one time he was coming down Ninety Mile Beach. Very few little trees growing along there, the odd one or two, there might be a fig tree here and there, but they're no good at all, there's mainly spinifex and grass. So this time when he

*Narrow passageway for livestock, as one leading to a sheep dip

49

camped, all he could think of was to light a spinifex and put the billycan in that. When that burnt out, he'd go and light another one. When he got about a mile from his swag, his camp and that, that billycan started to boil. He put his hand into his pocket to get the tea leaves and he found out he'd left it behind at the camp. So, he had to walk right back there, about one mile to get the tea leaves. By that time, the billycan water was cold again, so he had to start off another one. Anyhow, he got it boiling and made the tea, but he couldn't drink it because it was terribly smokey!

Old Dobson never worked. He used to tell us that he had a radium mine. He said, "It's something terrible-size! It's out here, about fifty mile out in the desert."

We were talking to him at Wallal Downs Station, while we were droving.

He said, "No company will have enough money to buy it, not even the Bank of England will ever have enough, so I'll give it away — I covered it up."

"Oh, must be only a little one," somebody said.

"Oh no, it's big. It stands up twenty-five feet high! But I covered it, covered it up."

"Oh?"

When he got to Mulyie, he said to the manager, "Can I get some pumpkin, boss?"

"Oh yeah, you can help yourself if you take a bag."

So he got the biggest bag he could find, that was a chaff bag. He picked all sorts of vegetables, he could never eat them in six months, but he filled that bag right up! He could hardly drag that over to his camp, he couldn't carry it. He stayed there until after the vegetables got rotten and went from there to Marble Bar. He had no swag. He just had a dillybag, an empty one. I don't know how he lived. The only time he got a bit of tucker, food into him was when he got to some place. He'd cadge that. He never had any money to pay for it.

He used to spin a lot of yarns, tell many stories, all sorts of stories and make people believe they're true, you know. So, it was a pleasure to give him a feed or a bit of food to take him onto the next station or wherever he wanted to go. He used to camp where no one else would ever stay, among rocks and things, you know rubbish. He'd use a rock for a pillow or a bit of wood, anything like that. He died in Marble Bar. He starved himself to death, more or less. The only time he ever got a feed was when he'd come to some station. The store-keepers wouldn't let him have any unless he paid for it, but he never had any money. Dobson of Australia his nickname was. I knew him pretty well but I don't know where he'd come from. He was a thin, tall bloke. He could talk all sorts of funny yarns, stories. This is a long time ago. Well, that was the finish of him.

Horses, camels and donkeys but no money

Back at Marble Bar

In 1923, I was back home at Marble Bar, home. I kept on learning the Aboriginal culture. I could speak the languages and understand what they were saying. I learned the full routine. I was around about there until 1927. What I have learned in Aboriginal culture, I haven't forgotten.

My Aunty Dinah told me this story then. It is the true story because she was there.

In 1899, the nearest doctor then was either at Balla Balla or Roebourne, she wasn't quite sure about that. They got the doctor to come, him and a blackfella to pilot him through. They went to Braeside on a pack horse. When they left Balla Balla or Roebourne they came to Whim Creek, then from Whim Creek to Croydon, Yandeyarra and Woodstock. From Woodstock they went to Tamborah and then to the Cooglegong Hotel, to Warrawoona, and Twenty Ounce and then straight to Braeside.

My father in Aboriginal way, was getting the crowd together to kill Hodgson. He'd been very cruel to him. First thing in the morning as soon as they could see, they surrounded the house. It was a two-storey building made out of bush timber and corrugated iron, of course. On the bottom of the stairs there was a cattle dog, a very savage one, tied up. They walked up and just killed him with a wakuburu, a fairly long and thick lump of wood.

Then they walked upstairs to get to the room where they thought Hodgson would be, but Dr Ed Vines was the first one to put his head out, he didn't know anything. As soon as my old fella saw this whitefella's head, he jammed in there and killed him stone dead, but he was sorry afterwards. He wasn't after the doctor at all, he thought that was Hodgson. Hodgson jumped through the window somewhere and escaped. Anyway, my father went around and Mrs Hodgson then walked out and he cried for her, you know. He was very very sorry over it.

Mrs Hodgson was going to have a baby. That's why Dr Vines was there. So my mother and her sister, that's Dinah, Dinah Carpenter, packed some flour, a billycan of water and some tea and they walked along with Mrs Hodgson for about five miles to a place called Lambing Creek, Thinggaraganya. Mrs Hodgson said, "This whitefella is plenty sick and tired fella" — that's how they talked them days. So they lay down under a big tree and Mrs Hodgson had the baby there. My mother lay on this side and my aunty on that side, in case of trouble during the night.

Next morning, when the morning star was still in the sky they got up. There was no one around. They weren't looking for them, those men. They only were after Mr Hodgson. Well they walked all that day. My mother and aunty carried the baby and a few belongings. Mrs Hodgson was sick. They lay down again.

Next morning, they woke up at piccaninny dawn. They were only about four miles out of Warrawagine and they walked to the homestead and left her there. They don't know what happened after that.

The police found out. They got my old man, my stepfather, my father in Aboriginal way, and took him and locked him up in Roebourne Gaol. They were to hang him. The next morning, the warden took his breakfast in. The door was still locked. He opened the door, but Bandy-Jim wasn't there. They don't know how he got out or where he got out. There was no sign of anything. He just got out, vanished. Later, he caught up with his fellow friends and my mother at Meentheena Station, not the homestead, but where they were camping. His wife, my mother was living with another man by then, so my old fella, he got a big spear and he said, "Oh, that's for you."

He speared my mother's leg and the other man's leg and said, "That'll fix you." So he got mum back. The police never found him.

I went with the Thompsons, driving camel teams at Marble Bar. We used to go out to cart wool and take the groceries out. I'd known them for a long time. We were all kids together. They had camel teams and the old man had a blacksmith shop. He was a blacksmith by trade.

When old Billy Thompson came here, there was no Port Hedland. He came to Condon on some ship, I don't know what ship. He couldn't get a job there straight away, so they walked up the Oakover River until they got to the junction, that's the Coongan, Coongan River.

Billy Thompson carried his son, young Billy on his back and his wife was carrying a billycan and a bit of tucker. They took their swags up the river and headed for Marble Bar. There was plenty of water all the way up the Coongan River. They got to Marble Bar and started this blacksmith shop, old

Billy did. That must've been somewhere around about 1880 or something like that. Everything been good ever since. He never looked back. Of course a blacksmith with wagons was a very important man those days.

As time went on, they got a few camels together and three wagons. One wagon was donkeys, a donkey team, and the other two wagons was camel teams. They had a few more sons by then. Billy was the eldest, then there was Rod Thompson and Don Thompson, that's the other brother. Well, Don Thompson, he pulled on bookkeeping and became a storekeeper; going trading clothes and food to different places out in the belt, you know, everywhere. Young Billy, the first boy, he started a station, Split Rock, a sheep station. The other boy, Rod Thompson, he pulled on anything, whatever he could get hold of, any job at all until he got married. Then, when the war broke out in 1914, young Billy and his brother Rod joined up to go overseas and fight.

They came back later on in 1919 when the war ended. They were alright. The fourth eldest son was Joe Thompson. He started on any job he could get hold of. Then, the next one was Sandy Thompson, he did the same thing. He worked anywhere and everywhere until they got the camel teams together and he started driving, carting cargo out to different places. Alf Thompson got a camel team too, and they went carting cargo, wool and stores everywhere, to all the stations as far as Ethel Creek.

They're all Billy Thompson's sons. The Thompsons had also a donkey team and that was lead by a big half-caste bloke called Dugal Cornish. He used to drive that, carting things to different places. Then there was Jack Thompson, that was the baby boy, he stayed with the father in the blacksmith shop until he got old enough to run a bit of a business. He worked in a shop at Nullagine and out at the Five Mile and back to Moolyella. He got married and he died. They're all dead now. They were the first settlers in Marble Bar.

The Thompson's were alright, you know, they'd been brought up with the Aboriginals. We used to cart wool with camel wagons from the Talga and Bonney Downs into the Coongan Sidings and put it on the railway trucks there. We had a lot of places to go to, you know. It kept us pretty busy there for a while. We were not getting any money for it, but *they* were getting paid alright. All around Yarrie, Muccan, Ettrick, Warrawagine, Callawah, Talga and Eginbah, they all had sheep, plenty of sheep.

At that time, about seven thousand people lived all around the district, around Marble Bar and Nullagine. There was no motor cars. All the transport they had was horses, camels and donkeys, but they made money.

There were quite a few Afghans. They had camel teams, old Nick Mohammed, he had a camel team. He used to do the carting to Marble Bar. There was Sid Mohammed and Mamajong, they all had camel teams. We worked for them in the young days. They were good people. Then there was Mula, old Mula Sid Mohammed, he had a string of pack camels, eighteen of them.

He used to hock fruit around the district. He'd cart cargoes from Condon to Marble Bar. Every afternoon, he'd lay his silk mat on the floor and pray. That's what I and all used to see him do, praying all the time. I think he must've been some sorta priest too. Old Inja Injaru, Jim Malkan and old Sarin had a bit of a wagon and used to cart wood. All little jobs around about the place. Old Kulalam, he was another, he used to cut wood and cart it on pack camels.

Old Sid Marter, he was a priest. He'd ride around on his old camel everywhere, anywhere that other Afghans were doing church work, you know.

Then there was old Zarene, he had a lot of fowls. He got killed by some foreigner, I don't know, some called him Matama. They say that this Matama had dug a deep round hole, about four feet down, and buried Zarene in it. Then he got a bucket of wheat and chucked it all over the grave and let the fowls go there to smother the tracks up. That was the end of old Zarene.

Then there was Abdul Cater, he had a little light camel wagon. He used to do a little bit of carting too, not very much. He lived on nothing, little or nothing, you know.

Some of these Afghans'd take their turban off and put a hat on. This one fella used to go out with the slaughterman and when the slaughterman shot a bullock or a sheep, he'd go and cut its throat. They weren't allowed to eat it otherwise. They wouldn't touch kangaroo, they wouldn't eat it because it has five fingers. They'd say, "He like a man that fella, he no good, he got five fingers."

They wouldn't have a bar of that and they wouldn't have bacon either. If they saw a pig in the yard, they'd just run away. This one fella, Jim Malkan, he was inside of a room. There's a few pigs around there walking about and one pokes his head through the door. Jim Malkan spotted that. Oh gee, he nearly went mad! He reckoned the devil was coming in!

They wouldn't cart any bacon or pork, they wouldn't touch that. A white storekeeper tried cunning ideas on another Afghan that had a string of camels. He put a side of bacon in a long case, the size of a side of bacon, a full side of bacon. This case must've been a bit weak because when the Afghan got along the road a bit, it busted a little bit. He noticed that bacon in there. Well, he just cut the line off that camel and left it there. He wouldn't touch it.

Those days, you'd get half a side of bacon in a sorta linen bag. It had an advertisement on it, a picture of a piggy. Now, one afternoon, I remember this as well as anything, old Nick Mohammed went and asked Martin for a bag of oats.

"Well, alright Nick, I'll go and get you a bag of oats. You stop here."

So he got this pig bag and he put the oats in that and of course he threw it at him, "Here you are Nick."

Old Nick saw this pig on the bag and gave it a kick. "You can keep your dirty rotten bag, I don't want it." Yeah, oh they wouldn't have that!

They're very strict that way. Every sundown, they'd all go and wash their mouths, their fingers, everything and they'd all pray on their mats lying on the floor.

We used to travel with them from Marble Bar to Nullagine or further out to Roy Hill way, carting cargo for different places. During three months of the year, they never eat in daylight. It's always before the sunrise or after the sun goes down. They drink water alright, but never eat.

In ordinary times, their main diet was curry. They made their meat all curried up, it was a lovely taste. We used to eat with them. They're very clean with their tucker, very clean! They'd lay a big groundsheet out and then a great big dish full of curried beef. Well everybody had to wash their fingers, their hands. You wasn't allowed to use a knife and fork or anything like that to get that meat out.

You got it out with your fingers. Everything was done by fingers. They had tea, a very good tea, and bread. They'd make their flat jacks* every meal. They had it fresh all the time. They'd never keep it stale or anything like that. You'd just roll them up and carry them in your pocket, tender as anything! They'd get plain flour and they put cream of tartar and soda in it. Well, everybody did that, but not the way they made it. They made it very thin and it was soft. You could eat it, no trouble at all. It was good tucker and they were very good cooks. While they was about you'd never starve, oh no!

They'd chew tobacco. They'd mix their tobacco up. They'd dolly it up and damp it with water. They'd get this lime and mix that up, fill up a jar with a top on it and they'd put it in their pockets. They'd get a pinch of that every day, every

*Small, flat usually leavened bread forming a pocket, which can be filled with food c.f. flapjack

meal, whenever they want it and they rub it on their teeth. Of course some of these blackfellas did that too, but they were different though. You'd never see them getting into arguments or anything like that, they were very good, very good people.

One day I went out looking for camels for my boss where I was working. Anyhow, I got to their place just after dinner and old Nick Mohammed said, "You had dinner Jack?"

I said, "No."

"Well," he said, "Hop into the kitchen, help yourself."

So I did. There was a lovely bit of meat there and flat jacks. I had a real good feed! I thoroughly enjoyed it. After I had lunch, he said, "Oh well, you've had a feed Jack?"

I said, "Yeah."

"Oh, what do you think of it? That's camel meat. It broke his leg, you see. He's a young one," and of course they had to shoot it.

Yeah, that was in Marble Bar.

The Afghans were at Marble Bar until 1924, before the trucks came in. When the trucks came in, there was no work for them. All them fellas left, barring Abdul Cater, he didn't go, but he wasn't Afghan.

Some went up north to Derby and Wyndham where there was no vehicles, motor vehicles, and I think a lot of them left Australia.

She's half round, half square and crooked

They'd be broke before they got anywhere

I went out to Hedland then. We were all after buffalo grass seeds. We would go out with a yard broom to get a few bob. We had a couple of seventy pound sugar bags each. We'd take the yard broom to sweep up all the seeds. Whatever we could get, we'd take to the butcher, old Joe Moore. He used to give us seven and six a bag.

The Esplanade Hotel was run by Mrs Mannion then, and next to that was a Greek shop and then the State Shipping Service — Wilsons. Then next to that was the Pier Hotel, which was owned by Mrs Pilkington and next to that there was a barber shop. They called this old fella Kudu Kudu, that means short fella. I don't know if that was his right name or not. Next to that was a Chinese laundry in Richardson Street.

There was a hotel on the corner of Richardson and Wedge Streets, the Crameri, and straight across the street, there was a courthouse — it's the Commonwealth Bank today. On the other side of the street was the Union Bank and next to that was a cafe owned by a Greek family, Paspalas and next then was the post office. There was three or four shops along there, one was a jewellery shop but I don't know who owned it. Right on the corner, where the National Bank is now, there was a drapery shop. It was owned by Athol Moseley and his mother. Straight across the road was the police station, where it is today, but it was a different building though!

Across Anderson Street was a Chinese storekeeper. He had a store where he sold anything, food you know, mainly all tin food — old Aug Qua was his name. Then there were no more buildings on that side after that store but on the other side, there were buildings, a butcher shop, old Joe Moore — in Edgar Street. Next to him, old Charlie Bayman, the carpenter and when you went up Richardson Street, the next building was the doctor.

I don't know what doctor it was then, but after him it was Doctor Vickers. He was the first Flying Doctor here and his pilot was Max Campbell.

The hospital was close to where the new hospital is now. There's only the remains of it there now. That was the end of town. There was no buildings further up. Straight down from the hospital, there was another Chinaman who also had a store there. They called him Ah Tow.

There were a few carpenters in town. There was old Charlie Bayman. Harry Oldfield, he was the carpenter for the railways. Another carpenter, Bob Anderson, the Anderson Street in Hedland, that's named after him. They called him Tiddlywinks. Then there's another carpenter, he used to go anywhere and everywhere with horse and cart, George Amber.

There was one old fella here. They called him Jack Webster. He saved up and saved up and bought a truck. When he got that paid off, he bought a refrigerator, a kerosene refrigerator. He was going to go prospecting. He came into Port Hedland, he got a case of beer and he put it down alongside the truck. He made his bed on a mattress alongside of that on the ground. Then he stayed there until he drank that case of beer. There's forty-eight bottles in a case. They're the big bottles those days.

When he woke up, he went and got some more. When he woke up again, he was stony-broke. See, he'd sold the truck, so he stayed there until he drank that dry. I think he got about five hundred quid for the truck and when he cleaned that up, he had nothing, only his swag, blankets and things like that. He went and sold that too. All he had was a mattress.

From there, he got a job when he got right. He wasn't a bad cook, a pretty good cook. He was a good all-round man. As soon as he got more money, he did the same thing again. He could never ever knock off, give it up. But as a person he was as good as anybody else. It was only the grog, the alcohol that had him beat, but as for talking to anybody when he was sober, and doing anything, he was just as good as anyone else. He was very good.

There were a lot of old fellas like that here, all the same sorta business. They couldn't give that alcohol up, they couldn't even save up enough to go to Perth for a holiday. They'd be broke before they got anywhere. The pubs did alright from them.

It was then, in 1924 when Keith McKay was killed. He owned Mundabullangana, and down at Nelsons Point the plane just went down, straight down, just like that, into the sea. Just behind the jetty and the Mt Newman Works, you know. Len Taplin, he was the pilot but he got rescued and McKay died. He was learning to speak Aboriginal.

I know a lot of white people, who I used to be with and used to be on stations or somewhere else, could speak Aboriginal languages just as good as the Aboriginals. Elma Corboy, she'd be one of them. She is dead now, but her and I used to play together when we were little. In 1905 I was born and she was born in 1901. It must've been somewhere around about 1907 when we were playing together at Mt Edgar Station — round that period like, you know, somewhere around about that. Old Maurice McKenna, he was the one who took Mrs Corboy and her little daughter, that's Elma, out to Meentheena because the old Corboy himself just went away from Mt Edgar. What for, I don't know.

So they went out to Meentheena with Maurice McKenna and in 1923 Elma got married to Kingsford-Smith. I was invited to the wedding from Elma.

The train leaves here Wednesday morning. Thursday they stayed up there in Marble Bar. There's trucks to be unloaded and loaded. Well, that was the day they got married. We was late. We came there on the Friday. The train was just ready to take off. We said goodbye to Elma and Kingy. That's the first time I seen him. Then they went to Perth. They got one boy.

Kingy took on the flying up here, up the coast here with Captain Brearley and Len Taplin. They were the first lot, the pilots on this coast, you know. The old Dragons they had the first; well they were the first lot, them three. They used to go as far as Derby, I think it was, and back.

I went and worked on Limestone Station for some time for old Tommy Mallett, doing a bit of butchering, you know, helping the butcher, old George Billet and doing station work. Then I went and worked on Corunna Downs Station for a long time with a bit of a break, you know, a change. When one place ran out of cash, I'd get a job somewhere else. The boss at Corunna Downs, Foulkes Taylor, was a terrible hungry man. He didn't care about feeding anybody much, not good tucker anyway. We'd just live on bread and meat all the time, that's all…bread and meat and black tea. We thought that was the best we could get and we had to eat it or else go hungry. There was quite a team of us. There must've been about twenty-five of us working there.

It was mainly cattle and sheep work but I had to learn anything and everything. I had to learn breaking in horses, donkeys and camels, doing windmills, sinking wells, putting up fences, repairing old fences and mustering. You had to do blacksmithing too. Those days you got two pieces of iron, you'd put them in the fire, weld them together and round them off on a crate. Anything like that, you had to learn, that and a little bit of motoring. That is, when the motors came in of course!

The right way to run a sheep station or any station is this: after the flood waters, the first thing to do is fix up your boundary fence. The wash-aways, fix all that up so your sheep don't get out and your neighbour's sheep don't get in, all that, like that. When that's finished, secured, you go and fix up all the waters, dry season windmills, pumping wells and also tanks, leaking tanks and leaking troughs.

Somewhere around about April, the lamb marking comes on. You mark all your lambs and fix them up in each paddock. Then your division fences, like boundaries, you cut it all up in sections so your sheep don't get mixed up, say wethers, rams, lambs, ewes, all that sorta thing.

Then you start mustering for shearing. When that's finished, the shearers are there and they shear the sheep. On average there are around about eight or nine shearers and they've all got separate pens. You count the sheep from each pen separately. Then you sort them out. Young sheep, old sheep, male or female. You draft them out and you count how many sheep you going to put in the different paddocks. You might put four thousand or five thousand in one paddock — it all depends on the size of the paddock — and about the same in the next one, but different type of sheep, you know.

When that's finished, everybody goes for a holiday. The work's done for that season. Of course there's a few people that stay on the job, like the windmill man and the manager or somebody like that, you know, important people, but the musterers they're all gone. They're all gone, might be a month or six weeks. They can go where they like and if they want to come back, they can and if they don't, well their manager gets a new lot of men.

If there is any cattle on the station, they'll muster the cattle up, do the branding and fix those up that need fixing. They'll do that in about February. When that's finished, they wait for the winter to come and start off with sheep again. There might be ten, twelve men on the job. The shearing starts over again.

That's how a good station runs. They don't all do it, because they're not good managers, you understand, young fellas. Well, there was three Jacks: Champagne Jack, Sunburnt Jack and Rock-cake Jack.

For a start, Sunburnt Jack was always on Bamboo Springs Station, you know, rouseabout, yardman and all that sorta thing. So, old Alec Beart, he wanted a well sunk. So he asked old Jack, Sunburnt Jack, if he could sink the well.

Sunburnt Jack said, "Yeah, that's nothing to me but I have to have a mate."

"Oh well, when you get a mate, might get one anytime, then I'll take you out and show you where I want the well sunk."

"Right."

A couple of days later Champagne Jack rolled along. He was pushing his motorbike — although that motorbike was still going! The engine could be started up, but he'd never ride it. He'd just walk alongside of it. So anyway, Champagne Jack got to Bamboo Springs and he and Sunburnt Jack knew each other. He was a Norwegian, old Sunburnt Jack. I don't know what Champagne Jack was. I think he was a Sandgroper, a West Australian.

"Yes, we will sink the well," said Champagne Jack.

So they went and seen the boss, old Alec Beart.

"Oh, that's very good," he said, very pleased.

"Well, I'll take you out this afternoon and show you where I want the well and also tomorrow I'll take all your gear out, windmill barrels, stands and all that sort of thing to sink the well. All the gear."

So they went out next morning with all their camp gear and all that to sink a round well. They wanted a round well you see. It went down good for about eight feet, soft ground, all pick and shovel work, but then it got hard. They had to drill holes and put dynamite in it. So they did that. Champagne Jack was the one that was doing the job down below. Sunburnt Jack was on top. He was on the brace as they call it.

Champagne Jack sang out, "Well you can make up the charges now Jack and send them down. I'll charge her up and let her go."

"Righto," Sunburnt Jack said.

He made up the charges and sent them down in the bucket. So Champagne Jack charged them all up and sings out to Sunburnt Jack, "Hey, you can pull me up now Jack."

"Yes, alright."

So he pulled him up and Sunburnt Jack says, "Did you light 'em?"

"No, it's too dangerous."

Sunburnt Jack said, "Oh well, I'll get a long handle shovel and dig up a bunch of spinifex and send it down. Don't light that one, we'll get another one, light it and chuck it on top of that one."

So, they did that. They went half a mile away. Boom. Way she went off, all went off together.

They didn't know whether they all went off or not, you know. So, they didn't go near the well that day. They walked over the camp listening if there was anymore, but nothing.

When they did go over to have a look, there was two wells instead of one! You know, too much fracture and the walls fell in. Well, they had to clean all that out and they'd start off again.

By that time, Rock-cake Jack come along. He was looking for work. They knew him. They asked him, "What about coming out and doing a bit of cooking for us?"

"Oh yes, that's my trade."

"Oh well, that'll do, a bit of tucker's nice after you done a day's work."

"Yes, that's right, smoko and that."

So, Rock-cake went out with them and started cooking. The other two were sinking the well. They bored some more holes and charged it up.

Sunburnt Jack said, "We'll stick a master fuse on this lot this time, and we'll get a long fuse about one hundred and fifty feet long so we can light it over there, instead of coming around and mucking around the well."

"Yes, that'd be a good idea," Champagne Jack said.

Away they went. It took a while for the fuse, you know, to go down the well. One hundred and fifty feet out there and about ten to twelve feet down. Way she went off! Well, that was good, this time they'd had sense enough to cut the fuses all different lengths, about two inches different.

"Oh, that's a good job."

Anyhow, the next day, after they'd cleaned it out, it started to get damp with water.

"Oh, we struck water just about!"

Anyway while that was going on, the boss come up and he had a look.

"Oh yeah, down a fair bit."

"But," he said, "That well is not really round."

"No," Champagne Jack said.

The boss said, "It's a half round, square bugger!" He said, "How am I going to get the cylinders down there?"

"I don't know," Champagne Jack said.

"Because she's half round, she's half square and crooked," he says.

"It's a funny well."

"Oh, never mind, I'll pay you. You're down the depth anyhow."

"How much water down there?" the boss said to Champagne Jack.

"Oh a lot of water, if you sit there, you'll get drowned."

"Yeah?"

There was only two inches of water in it! They'd only just struck water! It had no depth in it, but it covered the floor. The boss didn't go down to inspect it. He stopped up on top and had a look.

"Oh yeah, I can see the water there," he said and so he paid them off and old Rock-cake made another cake. He used to make cakes and things. But the cakes was that hard, you couldn't bite them! Like rock, you had to break them up with a hammer!

So anyway, they split up and that was the end of that story. Old Champagne, he wouldn't ride the motorbike, because he reckoned it wouldn't pull when he got on it!

Now, I want to tell you about the people and places around the area. Mundabullangana, that station down there, was owned by McKay. Then next to that is Yandeyarra, Jack Stanley was there a terrible long time. Back this way on Indee Station, was Rob Edkins. Sheep stations, they're all sheep stations. At Wallareenya, there was Charlie Kerr, that had sheep too; Pippingarra — Peter Richardson — that had sheep; Tabba Tabba Station — Alan Crawford; Strelley — Corney and Hardey; Shaw River — Hardies and Mitchell. They're all sheep stations. Carlindie was owned by McGregor and Riches. Lalla Rookh was owned by Harry Coppin and Ted Jefferies, that was a sheep station too.

De Grey Station originally was owned by Tom De Grey. He was the man who took the country away from the wild. He sold out to Mr Padbury. Padbury sold out to Grant. Grant had it for quite a while, then he sold out to Mark Rubin. My uncle was working there for years — Billy McPhee.

When you go up the river there is Mulyie Station, that was owned by Angus Campbell and then sold out to Mark Rubin who owned all of them along there. Ettrick Station was owned by George Corney and George Hardie. Mark Rubin bought it in the end. Pardoo Station was owned by Frank Thompson. Nimingarra Station was owned by Ben De Marchi. Muccan Station by Mick Corbett and Charlie Holthouse, Yarrie Station was owned by Herbert and Bill Coppin. Warrawagine was owned by the Ball brothers and Michael Corbett. Tom and Ted Hardie owned Warralong Station, mostly sheep, but a few cattle too up top, not many though. Frank Welsh was the manager there. Bungalow on the Coongan river, that was run by the Robinsons, four of them, four brothers. They lived on bungarras they tell me. That's goannas. They had a pub too, the Coongan Pub. That was run by the other brother, Conrad Robinson.

Eginbah was owned by Harry Coppin then. There were quite a few fossickers around. They had all funny sorta names. There was Musical Tramp — his real name was Billy Keanon — and there was Dollypot, that was his nickname, Dollypot. Every bit of stone he found, he dollied it. He used to pick up stones anywhere and everywhere and dolly it to see if there's any gold in there. So they called him Dollypot. Some called him Four-By-Two, I don't know his proper name. Four-By-Two, he was two inches tall — two foot high — and about four foot across this way. Well, that was Bamboo Creek.

Bamboo Creek is sixty-five kilometres east of Marble Bar. There was a state government battery there and also a post office. Old Pickard was running the post office and the mine. The blackfellas used to call him Pickarse.

"Yeah, I'm gonna go see old Pickarse."

The Bulletine was Woodmans' — Mr and Mrs Woodman. They had a son called Billy. The Prophecy Goldmine was owned by Bert Watson. Next to that was Bonneydoon. Anybody used to work that show. The Charlie Goldmine was owned by McAllister. Kitchener Goldmine was owned by Huey Jackson. Old Bill Daily worked there. The Federation Mine was owned by Fred Wells. There was an Italian out there, Micky Tanderlini. His mine was named after him, Micky Two. He wasn't a bad old chap, but he didn't do any good there, so he went into Marble Bar. He was working in there on some shows, any show at all to get a crust. He then worked the Homeward Bound Mine, not far from the State Battery.

There was one fella there who camped in one of the tunnels, Walter Myers. Another dingbat. He was a pensioner. The pension wasn't very much those days. It might've been only two pound ten a week or something like that. He'd get a plug of tobacco, four ounces and cut it up. Then he'd go around the bush picking up leaves. He'd crush it all up and mix it up with the tobacco. Instead of havin' one plug of tobacco, he'd have about three. He'd smoke that. You could smell him from half a mile away.

Now we come to Talga Station. Now, that was the Green brothers, Fred Green and Harry Green and Frank Walsh. Limestone Station was owned by Tommy Mallett and all the Moolyella Lead on the McDonald Flats was owned by Mick O'Leary and Billy McDonald. They used to get their cargo from Condon on pack camels and take the tin away with pack camels back to Condon. That's before Port Hedland. When Port Hedland opened up, well of course they just carted it in to the railway station at Marble Bar, you know, put it on the railway there. We're out at Marble Bar now.

The biggest family at Marble Bar was the Thompsons. There was the police station, post office and the courthouse all in one, all joined together sorta business, all in one building. The policeman was Corporal Strapp. Old Frank Williams, he was the Postmaster, and there was a Residential Warden, old Warden Ritchie. Well, we had a chap there, they called him the Red-arsed spider — that was his nickname. His name was Bob Turner. He had a bicycle shop. If we wanted a bicycle for the weekend, we'd give him five bob, we could have it for the three days. The storekeeper, that was Andy Shanley and Albert Hanson. He was a Norwegian, I think. He was a good fella.

There was also a bank there, the Union Bank, but I don't know who was the boss there. There was so many change-overs. I knew one chap was there, his name was England. Then there was old Parson, I can't remember his full name. George Miles, he bought two stores, one was owned together with Billy Maher. He had the store and he had the pub too. Another pub right across the road, the Marble Bar Hotel, that was owned by Andy Elliot. Next to that was a food shop too, old Tom Matthews.

I never went to school because there was no school to go to those days, no school in Marble Bar. White people that had children, sent them down south, down to Guildford or Perth. Most of those children was in Guildford, a big school there. The little bit of what I learned about reading and writing, I picked up from the writing on tins, jam tins or any tins at all. I'd go to my white mate, "What does this say?"

"Oh, that says jam tin, J–A–M, jam."

"Oh yes."

So that's how I got along.

The Shire Council then was called the Road Board and the man that was running it was Jack Scrymgour. I think he was running two jobs, Water Supply and also Roads. Second in charge was George Chessman. I was working under him later, he was the boss too. They used to keep all the water in good order those days, you know, government wells, somewhere about ten or fifteen miles apart.

There are three big pools around Marble Bar: the Marble Bar Pool, Chinaman's Pool and Magazine Pool, which is about two miles out. You can get plenty of water in them. They go dry with the drought but you can always get water in the sand. You only have to dig for it in the shallow. There are lots of nice places.

There was quite a few families there. There was two lots of Snells. One Snell went mining with all his boys and the other Snell started a camel team. He was all over the place too. He had a place out at Mt Governor, that's where Mt Newman is now. Then he went to Kumarina and started that up and from there to Lake Naberoo and Eladgie Springs. He had one son, he died out there. That was two families.

There was one fella out at Marble Bar at the time. I remember him well, old Ned Roche. They nicknamed him "Rum Taster". A lot of those old fellas used to be around the area. They was terrible on the grog, terrible. They went more for whisky, rum, brandy and gin, anything like that. Oh, they'd have a bit of beer for a start when they first come in. They'd drink until their pockets got empty. They wouldn't eat, because they were too drunk all the time. They was too drunk to eat any food. Mt Edgar Station was owned by Worner, Corboy and Taylor who sold out to Clarkson. Corunna Downs Station was owned by Drake-Brockman. Pilga Station was owned by Walter Goode. Hillside Station was all sheep and was owned by Doctor Gillespie. Bamboo Springs Station was owned by Arthur Beart, sheep station too. Warrie Station was Billy Luke. That finishes that area, Marble Bar area.

Now at Nullagine there was about 7000 people there, working gold at the Conglomerate. There were four pubs there, but I remember two. Walker owned the Conglomerate

Hotel, and the Nullagine Hotel was owned by Miles & Co. The policeman's name was Harry Crowden. Billy McGovern was the postmaster, Jack Hayes was a sorta Justice of Peace, or something.

The Conglomerate Mine, they used to water it down with the hose to get the gold out. They found a few little diamonds, very small, about as big as a match head. I don't know the exact spot where they came from, no one does, but they came from somewhere in those rocks. They found one diamond at the One Mile Battery too, out one mile from Nullagine. They found it in the corner of the box, where the battery stamp crushed the stones. It was there in the corner.

At Barton Goldmine, there was Mick Doherty and Maurice McKenna. At the Twenty Mile Sandy, a chap by the name of Tom Bayes, used to do the carting with horse drays and Bill Smith was another one.

Then there was Eastern Creek, there was Mick Doherty, Tom Masterson, Davy Guinness and they had one Afghan out there, Gooallan, out from Nullagine. They worked the show up on the top. They called it the Doherty's Reward and also the Morning Star. They used to cart the stones down with pack camels to the battery. That was the end of that.

Bonney Downs sheep station was owned by Stewart and Wehl. Fred Wehl and Jeff Stewart. From there to Roy Hill Station, that's cattle station now. Roy Hill was owned by Boonga McKay those days, early stages. In 1929, the Roy Hill Station was changed. Another mob took over, Jim Smith & Co. The manager was Tom Nelson that was in the 1920s. Ethel Creek was owned by old Charlie Smith and Mulga Downs by the Hancocks. Marillana was Nelson — Boondah was Hadley Good and Punch Liddelow — Balfour Downs was Alf Crofton and next to that was a government station, it was on a rabbit proof fence: Jigalong. Then from there to Murramunda Station — Ernie Shiloo. And across from there the Sylvania — Charlie Smith and nephews.

Down the Murchison (1927-31)

Wasted more time looking for work than getting some

In 1927, I went down the Murchison. There was no Aborigines there that could speak our languages. I was down there nine years. I went to Austin Downs out from Cue. I was with them doing all the cattle work, droving and also mustering all the time. I worked on the Ashburton for Arthur Meehan for quite a while, that's on Austin Downs and also Mt Vernon, the other station that belonged to him.

When Nannine town was going strong, on the other side of Meekatharra, about twenty-four miles from Meekatharra, there was a place called Belelle, named after the owner himself. It was about a mile north of Nannine. Harry Sprigg owned Annean at that time.

There's another place between that and Meekatharra, called The Gap. It's more or less an orchard, where they grow big oranges, Navel oranges. The chap that owned it those days, was Freddy Swinton. It's only a little place.

On the other side, on the east side was Yarrabubba, it was owned by two brothers, Ned Meehan and Alec Meehan. Back this way, there's a pub and there's a pool on the Stock Route called Saddlegunna. On the next creek, I suppose about fifteen miles away, they call that Nugglegunna. Then there was the other place going towards Peak Hill, Bryah, owned by Francisco, he was the owner. That was all around about 1927.

Next to that was Peak Hill town, goldmine. The State Battery crushed the stones. There was also a pub there, a police station and a butcher shop. In the butcher shop, the butcher's name was Robert Shakesburg, Jumbo, old Jumbo. One fella had a camel team, they called him the White Khan. But his proper name was Sammy Haggett. That's all Peak Hill.

Next to this Peak Hill, was another station called Gidgigunna, owned by Jimmy Howard. He had a few sheep on it, few cattle, horses. He was a married man. He had two daughters as far as I know. I never seen any boys.

Back towards Meekatharra, there's a place called Bilyuin Pool. There was a pub there, owned by Wally Lee. Glory Lee was his daughter, his wife was there too. He had a pub over in Holdens Goldmine, Holdens Find they called it. They had a battery there too. Bilyuin Pub on the Ward River, it was made out of mud. The pub, that's north of Meekatharra. Close to that was also a little place called Spring Vale. Billy Fisher owned it.

From there to Abbots Goldmine. Next to that was Garden Gully and next to that was a station, a pumping station for the town's water supply.

The next place was a bit of a station, it was a slaughter yard, it was owned by Bill McRae. In the early days, they called it Yoothapina Station. That's not far from Greenwood Station, next-door neighbour. Next-door to them was Sherwood, that was owned by Billy Nichols. They had sheep on it, a sheep station. Then you come back this way to Munarra Station, that was owned by Straker and Church.

There was a big mob of people at Tuckanarra, halfway between Meekatharra and Cue. There used to be a wayside pub there for the rail. The train used to go past there. Tuckanarra was a little bit of a township, not much. There was a hotel and a store. Not very many people lived out there permanently, might have been five or six. There were places all along that line those days. You'd go from Mt Magnet to Wandarrie and then to Day Dawn.

Day Dawn was a big mining town at one time, it was held by the German company, the Great Fingall. There is a tower there, you can go up and up and up. When you look down, a motor car looks like a little beetle! There were two big bull wheels up there.

They had horses working underground pulling the trucks, but when the war broke out, the Germans had to close the mine down. It was never worked after that and it started to fall in everywhere. There was a sand dump there, a mountain, a couple of hundred feet high, white sand that's been through the mill. You could see it from everywhere. Oh, there was a lot of people in Day Dawn those days. There was a pub there too. Day Dawn Hotel they called it.

The railway went on from there to Cue and Tuckanarra, and from there to Nannine and then Meekatharra. There was a place between that, I think they called it Yaloginda, but I don't know whether it was a town or not. There was a few buildings there. Austin Downs was real good. I was getting plenty of money and it wasn't hard work, easy work.

One time we had a mob of cattle to pick up at Nookawarra. It took us about four days to get there. We had only horses and carts and things like that, no motor cars. So we got the cattle and took them back to Austin Downs. That took us about ten, twelve days. There was five of us and I was cook for that lot. We were getting three pound a week!

When the Depression was on, a lot of people were working on the railway line doing relief work. They'd have a fortnight on and a fortnight off, women and kids and men, you know. It was something terrible!

The government had decided to build a big dam, the Meekatharra Dam, to keep the people going with food, you know. Well they'd also get two weeks on and two weeks off. They lived in tents and things like that. They had hardly any food. They were just plodding along. I don't know what wages they were getting, but it wouldn't be too much. It was just something to keep them alive.

Oh yeah, it was no fun. You had to be somewhere around about nineteen to twenty years old or younger to get a job. Anybody over that wouldn't be given a job because they were too old. Well you'd see them elderly people carrying their swags. Oh, they'd have their tobacco, tea, sugar and a bit of flour. People used to give it to them, you know. They couldn't buy it, pay for it because they had nothing to pay it with. The soles of their boots was worn out. Some of them had been to the 1914-18 war.

You'd see women going to the rubbish dump to pick up an old pair of shoes, people asking for a bit of tea or sugar to carry them on until they got a job somewhere. That's white people I'm talking about! It was very very hard. So it got hard where we was too.

Mr Meehan, the boss came to me one day, "Well Jack," he said. "I have to cut all the wages down to half, that's thirty bob a week. It's not only your wage, but everybody else's too. I can't do anymore than that. If you know anything better, you can go and when things get better, you can always come back here."

"Well," I said. "I'll go kangaroo shooting."

There was a few motor cars about, not very many, a few old Dodges and some Opels, that's a German make. There was a few from England, Thornycroft and Daimler, and some from America like Dodges and Chevs. You could buy a motor car for a hundred and fifty quid, a brand new one. They were alright too. I had a few bob in the bank, so I bought a T-model Ford and went to a few stores shopping. I bought a rifle and went out for kangaroo skins.

To start off with I had a white lad working with me, but when we got the first lot, two hundred, he got his share of the money and he wouldn't come out anymore. He got drunk and one thing and another like that, so I went out on my own after that. I went around Nannine, Cue and Meekatharra, all around those areas, those places.

I done alright. The Depression didn't affect me for a living then. I was getting thirteen pound a hundred, for a hundred kangaroo skins. Three and six a pound. It was quite good, self work, but I had to work! I used to get about forty, thirty-five or forty kangaroos a night. That was as much as you could handle. See, you got to skin them. Then you got to take the carcases, drag them away to where there's plenty of wood and destroy them, burn them. Then you come back and you peg your skins out and you got to trim them. Take the fat and bits of meat off the skin. When that's finished you got to turn around and cook a bit of food for yourself. By that time, it's about three o'clock in the morning. You might sneak a bit of sleep in, not too much, might be one hour. Then you go back to the trough, where they all come in for water.

In summer, they come in at about five o'clock or half past five. Then you start shooting again. You might do this for a couple of weeks until you get your bundles of skins, say two hundred. I didn't shoot anymore than two hundred each time, because I only had one car to carry the skins. I'd put them on the mudguard and take them into town to sell to Wesfarmers. If you hang onto the skins for too long, you have to paint them with weevil paint to keep the weevils away.

So, I got about twenty-six pound a fortnight, that was alright, good money. I had nobody to keep, only myself. Oh well, I had to pay for fuel, food and things like that. I lived that way on and off for a long time. It was very hard work.

I used to go into town for a break. I had a lot of friends in town, in Cue and also down at Day Dawn, it's only four miles apart. Anyway, with this T-model Ford, I was sitting up in the street one night in Cue and my friends came along. "Hey Jack, what about going down to Day Dawn?"

I said, "Yes, alright."

Two blokes had asked, but instead thirteen of them got on! Some on the mudguard and some on the top of it. Away we went on the gravel road down to Day Dawn. The pub then, was run by Charlie Darcy and Maudie. Anyway, we all got down there, some were drinking and some didn't want a drink and quite a few teetotallers. Oh, there were a lot of drunks too. The back seat would only carry three people at the most, but there was about six in there sitting on each other's lap! Aah — the good old times!

When we got to Day Dawn, I parked the car in a place and couldn't get it out again. The steering in that old T-model Ford was not like these cars you get today. It would only go around a little bit. I said, "I can't turn the motor car around and I can't see to go back because it's dark over there."

"Oh," they said, "Don't worry about that Jack. Four of us will get in front and four or five will get at the back and we'll carry it around."

That's what they did. Oh yeah, I'll never forget that.

When things started to get better, I went back to Austin Downs but they soon ran out of work again.

So I went to a place they called Lakeside Station, owned by the Clarksons, but I never worked there because it's too small. Another place near Cue, they called Yarraquin Station, was owned by Boddington. I didn't work there because they had no money to pay wages. There's Cogla Downs, that was owned by Beaton's family, they had no money either to pay anybody. So I asked for a job on a place called Taincrow. They had no money either. I tried all those places. They was all in the same boat, they had no money. They couldn't afford to pay, so I gave the game away, looking for work. Wasted more time looking for work then getting some.

I went out to Yarrabubba, they couldn't afford to pay anyone. That's a station, sheep, out from Meekatharra. I met a fella, tall blackfella, they called him George Coyle. He was a terrible man, he was an outlaw. He was alright with me, no trouble at all. We only just had a yarn, but he never tried to make any damage, you know, to me. They were after him, the police, all the time. He was in police trouble all the time. It didn't matter where he was.

One day he was at a place they call Mt Yagahong, it's out from Meekatharra and beside it there's a pub, not far. They called it Gabanintha. You see, the policeman knew he was there. He was hanging around that hill, Mt Yagahong, but they couldn't grab him, couldn't catch him, he was too quick. He hid behind the big rocks. He'd sit behind them. The policeman was down below. He knew he couldn't get in there so he fired at George Coyle. The bullet ricocheted back. George moved away unharmed. George never thought of killing anybody, you know, do damage or something.

Now old John Meehan caught him on his property one day and chased him. George Coyle was on foot but the horse couldn't catch him, he was too fast. So John lost him, but he was out to catch him all the time. You know, George used to go and kill a sheep and cook it and eat it. What he didn't eat, he'd throw away and kill another one. All that sorta thing. Things he used to do! Go into town, pinch a bit of tea and sugar and get away with it!

Old Charles Smith bumped into him once. Old Charlie had many stations. He had Ethel Creek. He had Bulloo Downs. He had Sylvania. He had Milgun. He had Greenwood. He was a sorta cattle king. I think he had a bit of a say in Munbinia too...I'm not too sure about that. That's out from Yalgoo, Yalgoo township. He was a good fella but a terrible mean man.

So one day, he'd come up to Day Dawn with his horses and his gear from Guildford, that's where his home was. He had saddles and pack saddles and all that, packbag. He'd leave them at Austin Downs and went away. When he come back on the train, he'd get off and first thing he does is go to the store, get a couple of pounds of sugar, a pound of tea, about eight pound of flour and a bit of salt. Go down to the rubbish heap, pick up a tin, a fruit tin for a billycan and a milk tin for a cup and he'd go out to the station, to Austin Downs and get his horses. Old John Meehan was his mate, sorta business, but they wasn't partners in anything. Old John Patrick Meehan was his proper name.

Anyway Charlie would start off. He'd get his three horses, two riding horses and one pack horse and he'd ride that to Greenwood, up to Milgun, Bulloo Downs, Ethel Creek and Sylvania. He'd inspect all these stations he owned.

So this time, he was going through Goldfields Well on Bulloo Downs, that was on the road where he used to go always. He'd never follow a main road, he'd go through the bush anywhere. No one ever knew where he was, when he'd get there, where he was going or anything. He'd never tell anybody anything. Oh, he'd tell the managers I suppose, the ones that run those stations for him.

Well this time he got back to Goldfields Well, pulling water up and watering his horses and his waterbag. He heard a shot go off up the creek, up near where people worked for gold. So he thought, "Oh well, this'll be very good. I'll go up and see 'em, have a bit of a yarn with 'em tonight."

When he gets there, just after sundown, there's two fellas skinning a bullock, one of them is George Coyle. Charlie pulled up, "G'day, how are you? Getting a bit of meat are yous?"

They said, "Yeah, we're getting a bit." They didn't know each other.

They said, "Oh, I think the bullock belongs to Charles Smith, but bugger him, he's got plenty."

Old Charlie replied, "Yeah, I suppose he has, that's alright. I might get a bit of steak off you for tonight. I'll chuck it on the coals."

"Oh yes, you're welcome, yes, yes."

He said, "I'll camp just over here, there's a bit of horse feed around here."

In the morning he went and got his horses, had his breakfast and packed up. He went over to these two fellas and said, "I'll pick up a bit of meat for the road now then mates."

They gave some to him and said, "You can take what you want."

"Oh, I only want a little bit," he said. "I'll get some more at Ethel Creek and Sylvania. They're bound to have some meat up there. Anyway, I'll think I'll push on," he said.

"I suppose, I don't know you boys, I don't know your names, but you know who I am."

They said "No, we don't."

"Well, I'm Charlie Smith. That bullock you killed there, that's mine. Never mind, I know it's hard to get meat, but next time you kill a bullock, kill a small one so you can take the lot. You'll never eat all that, that'll all go rotten and you'll throw it away."

"Oh."

"Yes, I own all these stations along here."

They didn't know what to do or what to say. Charlie Smith couldn't do anything. They were two against him, you see.

But that's what he told them. Yeah, he's a terrible mean man with his working people. The wages was only two pound ten a week those days. That was for the managers.

After he'd spent about five or six weeks at Ethel Creek and three or four weeks at Sylvania, he'd go to Bulloo Downs. He'd spend another three or four weeks there and go on to Milgun and stop there for another two, three weeks. Old Jack Skeen, he was the manager there. He was a good old fella. Charlie Smith he'd push on to Greenwood, only five miles out from Meekatharra town. He'd go from there to Austin Downs again and leave all his horses there. It'd take him about two days to go down, only seventy-five mile. He travelled like that every year. Sometimes he'd do it twice a year, old Charlie.

One of his friends said to him one day, "What are you gonna do with all your money, Charlie, when you die?"

"Oh well," he said, "I got two sons, they like money."

He said, "One fella likes speed boats and the other fella likes motor bikes and aeroplanes."

"Oh."

"So if they have the same pleasure in spending the money like I did making it, they'll be alright."

Old Charlie, he died. I worked for people that had worked for him and I know all them stations. Oh yeah, I worked on all them stations. I was there.

I didn't know his home in Guildford, but the boys, I knew them. Laurie and Jack. Laurie, he liked speed boats and aeroplanes too. The other fella, Jack, he liked motor bikes and aeroplanes and the money just went like water with them. They didn't worry about the money. Oh, they were good fellas too. They were different to him, different men altogether.

You never knew where you'd meet Charlie, no one ever knew, no one ever knew when he'd come along. He was out to catch his managers, watch how they're doing. If they were doing anything or doing something good, he'd keep them on. If they were doing something no good and not working, he'd sack them and get another manager. He was one of them sorta fellas.

He died at Nannine Trucking Yards, trucking a mob of bullocks on the train to the Midland Junction. He died on a bag of chaff you feed horses with. There were many bags of chaff, he lied on one of them and that was it.

I went around to Nannine town, started to look for a bit of gold. I didn't know anything about looking for gold, but I tried my luck. I didn't get anything. From there I got work at Mt Seabrook Station for Mick Campbell and Co. I was there about six months. They nearly went broke paying me thirty bob a week and keep.

Then there was Mileura, that was owned by the Walsh brothers. There was another station there called Madoonga, it was owned by a bloke by the name of Thorton Pearse. He couldn't pay anybody either, and there was another place called Beringarra, owned by New Zealand Pastoral Company. Nookawarra, that was owned by George Spalding, MacIntosh, Fry and Hancock. All cattle out from Cue. All these places I mention to you are all around Cue and Meekatharra.

After that, I went chasing foxes, they paid three quid a head for foxes at that time. It was good money, you know, for the foxes. They're hard to get. I was there around Cue for a while doing that sorta job. It was very good.

Another bloke there, a bloke by the name of Huey King, a half-caste chap, he had a young wife. He wasted more time looking after her than doing his job. He's watching us. We wasn't worried about her. He was a funny man, he was. He couldn't go anywhere unless he took her!

When we finished fox chasing, I went tin mining, dry-blowing out from Marble Bar. Done a fair bit of that. It was alright, a bit of tucker in it, wasn't much money. Tin was very poor price at the time.

There is a story

A family man

In early 1932 I went to Moore River Settlement. There was not much work anywhere, you know. People that had money were hanging onto it. They were frightened to employ too many people because they couldn't afford it. So I went down there, but wasn't getting any money, no wages at the Settlement. In 1932, I got married there.

I was twenty-four when I met up with my girl. I went from Meekatharra on the train, to Moore River, Mogumber Siding, the railway station and got off there. It was just break of dawn when we got there. Old Neville,* he was the first man to come up to me.

He said, "G'day."

I said, "G'day."

He said, "What's your name?"

I told him, "Jack McPhee."

"Where are you going?"

---

*A.O. Neville, Chief Protector of Aborigines 1915-40

"Oh," I said. "I'm going home to see my half brother over at the Settlement."

"Yeah?" he said. "You didn't get permission from me, did you? You know I can put you in jail if I want too."

"Oh well," I said. "I better catch the train and go home."

"Oh, you can go now."

My half brother walks up and Neville says, "Oh, here he is, you'll be alright. You can go out there but you've got to leave the girls alone. Don't run away with them!"

"Oh," I said. "I didn't come down for that purpose. I came down to see him." That's Moore River Settlement.

After I was there a while, my half brother said to me, "You should get married, you know. You could do alright out on them stations and wherever you are."

"Yes, well I don't know much about that. I, aah, you wouldn't be so free."

"Oh well, you get a good cook, you can both work. She can cook for the station and you working would be alright."

I said, "Alright then."

So that's how I started off and got married and got hooked up. I went and seen the superintendent out at the mission, the settlement.

"Yes, well we'll see about it. You see you can't just get married, tell me today and want to get married tomorrow. It'll take a while."

I said, "Oh yeah."

We had to wait six weeks, we got engaged and everything. Six weeks later we got married.

I got a job out from Meekatharra at a place called Mt Padbury. I knew the boss, Billy Martin, I knew him very well.

So, my wife did the cooking on the station and I done all sorts of work; breaking in horses and working sheep. Billy Martin had cattle too. I'd do any sorta job at all. We were out there for about twelve months.

I went droving with Billy Martin. We came up to Noreena Downs, went droving at Frazier Downs and got a mob of sheep, four thousand sheep. There was five of us in the team. I was the cook. It took us about three weeks to bring the sheep to Mt Padbury. When we got back and had everything settled again, my missus, she wasn't too happy in that place. We had a child by then. She wanted to get back to her mother, so I said, "Alright then." Billy himself had slackened off. He didn't have much money. I went and seen him and he said, "Yeah, that'll be okay."

I came to Prairie Downs, me and my missus, working for old Brumby Leake. I was there for about eighteen months. I met up with all these old fellas again and I learned a lot more of Aboriginal culture, like corroborees, things like that. I learned to use boomerangs and spears, all that sorta thing. I learned Nyamal and this other language, Palyku. They'd be the same, but a little bit of a difference in saying, you know, a little bit. Say, in Nyamal, "yamangarina" that means "go away, I'm going away" and in Palyku, he'd say, "Yanamanga" same thing, "Going away."

"Yuluwali" that means "Going home to his home, his camp" and in Nyamal he'd say, "Yamangarina yulugadai" — "He's going home his camp" too.

So that all got into my head and I've never forgotten it. I was with them all quite a bit, working all around since then. I learnt three Aboriginal languages, Nyangumarta, Nyamal and Palyku. Nyangumarta is a bit hard. But you've got to get used to it.

Anyway Brumby was very good. He was a very hard man in living conditions. He'd eat bread and damper or pea soup all the time. He'd make the soup with kidneys and tail. Oh, it was good too. He'd cook it up, yes. Oh, there are quite a few stories about him!

There is a story about Brumby Leake and Monty Benda. Brumby Leake owned a station, Prairie Downs. Monty Benda owned a station called Bald Hill. Brumby Leake was going to Meekatharra with a mob of cattle. When he got to Bald Hill, one cow had a calf, had a baby. So he said to Monty Benda, "You can have the cow and calf. I suppose you'll give me something for it one day."

"Oh yes, I'll give you ten quid."

"Okay."

The next time old Brumby went down there again, he had trouble with his horse. It had a crook foot. He said to Monty Benda, "You can have this horse, as long as you give me seventy quid for the horse the next time I see you."

"Oh yes, that's easy done. That's alright, Brumby."

Another time, later on, Brumby Leake went to Wiluna with a mob of cattle for the butchers. This time Monty walked up to old Brumby. Brumby'd had a few, a bit of this grog in him.

He said, "G'day Brumby."

"Hello Monty, how are you?"

"Aah, I just come to get that money I've lent you in town."

"Yeah?"

"That eighty quid."

Brumby said to him, "Well look, about that, that eighty quid you promised me for the cow and calf, and the horse...well look, you owed me for the cow and calf and you owed me money for the horse. The money that I borrowed off you in town, I've got it in my pocket and it's gonna stay there, you can have this. You can have Mrs Palmer and five daughters. These five daughters here!"[*]

Another time, old Brumby went out mustering in another man's country, on Bulloo Downs country. He found some cattle that wasn't his. The cattle belonged to Bulloo Downs Station. Judge Dwyer owned Bulloo Downs and the manager took the judge around, showed him everywhere. They came

---

[*]Palm and five fingers. A fist

to this little yard with this one cow that had five calves. They went to see Brumby. They knew it was him.

Dwyer said to Brumby, "Hello Brumby."

"Hello, I don't know who you are but I don't care either," said Brumby.

"Well, I'm Judge Dwyer," he said.

"Oh."

"Mr Brumby," Dwyer referred to him, "What's the idea of your cow havin' five calves?"

Brumby said, "Well I'm not responsible for that. They can have as many as they like."

So Dwyer couldn't do anything about the cross-branding. He just had to leave.

Old Brumby again. He took a mob of cattle into Peak Hill to the butcher. He brought in about twenty head to be slaughtered, you know. Anyhow, someone found out this cattle didn't belong to him. He was selling somebody else's cattle. They went and reported it to the Peak Hill Police. Brumby was married to an Aboriginal woman, old Mary.

Anyway the police came and arrested old Brumby, took him and put him in the lockup. Mary went to visit him. This cattle was already in the yard when Mary came to visit him. Brumby said, "I'm glad you came, Mary. When you go back to the camp, you open the gates and let them cattle go, let 'em go."

Right, Mary did that and chased them off.

The police had nothing on him, they had no proof. He got away with that, the police let him go!

Yeah, he was a very tricky man, old Brumby, Brumby Leake. Originally he'd come from Diamantina in Queensland when he was young. He started Prairie Downs. Oh, he was doing alright, it's only a small place but it was good. He lived hard all his life on bread and meat, bread and meat. He was good to everybody, you know, but he'd pinch a horse or cattle, bullock, cow, anything. When you'd ask him, he wouldn't know anything about it. He was pretty clever that way, so he got out of a lot of things. He died at eighty four. I don't know who he left the station to, I couldn't say, I was up here in Hedland.

One day, he said to one of his mates, "You better make a damper when you go to the camp, if you're early."

The bloke said, "Well, I've never made one before."

"Well," Brumby said, "All you do is pour some flour in the dish, put some water in it and put it in the fire."

"Oh yes."

So the bloke didn't know what he meant by putting it in the fire sorta business. He didn't ask. He just chucked the dough and all in the fire. The flames went anywhere. When Brumby come along, he asked, "Where's the damper?"

"Oh," the other one said. "I put it in the fire, it all got burnt up."

"How do you mean, you put it in the fire and it all got burnt up? Didn't you dig a hole and bury it?"

"No, you didn't tell me to do that."

"Oh well, we got no damper for supper. We'll have to eat just meat tonight."

"Yeah well, I didn't know. I never made a damper in my life," the other bloke said.

"Yeah but," Brumby said, "You know how to eat them, don't you?"

"Yeah, I can eat them alright. They're nice too."

"Yes, well you dig a hole in the ground in the ashes and cover him up. Make him stiff, not watery. Make him stiff and push the fire on one side and cover him up in the hot ashes and sand."

"Oh, that's the way! I'll do that the next time, so we'll have tea then."

"Yes, that's alright."

Another time, old Brumby worked with a chap called Lindsay. He said to Lindsay, "You know anything about cattle, stockwork?"

"No," Lindsay said, "you'll have to show me."

"Well," he said, "you chase 'em and grab 'em by the tail and throw 'em."

"Oh yes."

"Don't get hold of the head because you won't be clever enough to get away from his horns. He'll poke you."

"Oh."

So alright. They went out and they seen a couple of mickies, young bulls, you know. This fella chased them and grabbed one by the two hind legs. It kicked him and knocked him out.

Brumby came along, "What's the matter Lindsay?"

"Oh, that young bull, he kicked me here and knocked me out."

"Oh well, that's your fault. I told you to grab him by the tail and throw him."

"Oh, I made a mistake."

"Yes."

It kicked him everywhere, in the guts and all.

Poor old Brumby, there are a lot of stories about him. I've forgotten most of them now. He was a tough old man. Worked with him for almost two years, but of course I knew nearly as much as he did, you understand. There were a few things I got from him and they were very handy. I didn't know as much as he did, but I knew how to handle stock and that's all he wanted. That was on Prairie Downs. I left him in 1934.

In 1934 I went up to the Oakover River and took up two blocks of land. Thirty-two thousand acres, one on this side of the rabbit proof fence and one on the other side. The one on the other side of the rabbit proof fence was very cheap, it was only two and six a thousand acres and on this side, it was fifteen bob a thousand acres. One place was called Marlu Marlu and the other block was Binbiyanha.[*]

*Near Balfour Downs country on the edge of the desert, about three hundred kilometres from Prairie Downs

We had cattle, twenty cows, four bulls and twenty-five head of horses, two camels and a dray. I was travelling with my wife, my eldest daughter Marie and my son Johnny. I was driving the cart with two camels and my daughter was in there with me. It was a spring cart, a big heavy thing. We hit a log in the sand and it sank down. We turned the blooming thing over! We went overboard, but weren't hurt.

So we took the two camels out of the cart and put them through on to the other side of the cart and pulled it over on its wheels again. Then we went along until we reached Skull Springs, that's where we was going to. My wife had been driving the twenty-five loose horses and Johnny was carried on the pommel of the saddle. We camped at Skull Springs.

The next morning we got up and started again. We went along about six mile and turned the cart over again, capsized and smashed one wheel up altogether. So, that was alright, that didn't stop us from travelling. We took the packs from out of the cart and put them on the camels. We left the cart there.

Then we went on about three miles I suppose, to a waterhole, a place they call Kulaluna. We camped there for a few days, not long, just spelling the horses.

Then we came to this Kurutjumaya. When I was on the Ashburton, Fred Mitchell told me this funny story about what had happened to him at that place.

Fred and his brother Jack Mitchell used to work on Roy Hill. They went for a holiday and they had two horses each and two pack horses. They went to Warrawagine. Their mother was still alive then. They went to Ethel Creek from Roy Hill and stayed there two or three weeks with their mother. Then they went up to the Oakover. They had one shotgun and they had one cartridge left.

They came to this place Kurutjumaya and the young fella said to the old fella. Jack said to Fred, "I'll go and catch that fella." He was in the soak, this kangaroo. Fred said, "Oh you can't handle him."

"Oh yes, I'm gonna try."

"We only got one cartridge. We might want that. We save that, we might get some ducks or turkeys up here."

So okay, Jack Mitchell went to sneak up to this kangaroo. Kangaroo in the soak. It's a hole they dig in the sand and they crawl in and they start drinking water.

So Jack grabbed this kangaroo by the tail, but this kangaroo come back and looked at him. The kangaroo got stuck into Jack. Jack punched him and kicked him and the kangaroo did the same. The other brother was laughing. He laughed and laughed. This fella was saying to him, "Get a stick and hit him on the head! Knock him out!"

So Fred went and got a stick. It was white ant eaten. It was only the shell of a stick. He went to hit this kangaroo but instead of hitting the kangaroo, he hit Jack!

Anyway, Jack had clothes on when he started, but when he finished he had no clothes on. The kangaroo'd ripped all them off him! All he had on was his belt. He had no trousers, no shirt, nothing. He had marks! The kangaroo biting him, kicking him and ripping him with his fingers, but they got the kangaroo in the finish.

The other brother'd got a solider stick and hit the kangaroo in the back of the head and killed him. They got the kangaroo but Jack Mitchell was sore, this young fella was. He was sore something cruel, I believe. He tried to save a cartridge. That happened somewhere in 1935. It was very funny, especially man fighting with a wild kangaroo. But you can get them, those kangaroos.

When I came to this soak with my wife and two children, we saw this kangaroo in there. I said, "Oh well, I'll walk up and hit him on the head with a stone."

I didn't grab him because he was a hill kangaroo, terrible strong fellas, them. So I walked up. I had this stone. The moment he got out of the water, out of this soak, I hit him on the forehead and I dropped him. I got him. He didn't get me. I was too cunning for him.

Yeah, things like that happen in the bush, you know. Anyhow, he was alright. We were looking for dingoes too. Didn't get any though, never got any. There was no dingoes about that time, they more or less on a holiday sorta business. Like tourists going around.

We went on to Meentheena. Charlie Blair and his family owned the station. He had five children. Keith, Thelma, Jean, Ian and Colin, they're a nice family. Those children, they had a governess out there, Miss Gilbert. When they finished school, these children used to help their mother and father. They used to go out and look for bush tucker, you know with a little tomahawk in their belt and a little billycan to get honey and some gum. They'd catch marandu, a bungarra, on the way and by the time suppertime came, they'd be all full, they didn't want any supper. They got honey and all that, you know, all the bush tucker. They got bardies too, they were very helpful, very good kids.

I never worked with them on Meentheena, but I was in and out there all the time you know, all the time. I was very close to them. I left my horses out there in the paddock on Meentheena Station. From then on I was there often looking after my horses and going out looking after our interest, our cattle, you know, out on the Oakover and the Davis River, Skull Springs, Tarra Tarra, all in that country. Charlie Blair and his wife was battling sorta business. He built the place up until it was good. It was real good, there was nothing wrong with it.

I wanted to fix the cart, so I had to go into Marble Bar in a truck. Sam Matthews got some spokes for my cart. I came back with the spokes. Jack Doherty and I packed two camels up and we led them, walking all the time, thirty-seven miles to where the cart was broken down to take this wheel to get fixed up. It was a great big wheel, iron wheel, there was not much wooden parts left. It was all smashed up. It's very hard to believe how we got it on the camel, one camel. We brought it back to Eastern Creek and we put the wheel together there, all barring some fellings[1].

I had to cut bush timber for that, timber they call Mountain Gum, good timber. So we did that, took it to old Jimmy Craig, he was a pretty handy man. He did it up. When we had the complete wheel, we put it on the camel again and took that out. We had to walk of course, up to where the cart was. It took us about a day or a bit more than a day.

Then we picked up the cart, put the wheel on it and came back to Eastern Creek. It was very rough, there was no road. Finally, we got back to Meentheena Station. We picked up the women and the kids there and took them back to Eastern Creek. We were there for a few days. We had our own time. We were working for nobody. So we went out to Lyndon, prospecting for gold. There is a lot of gold if you can find it. It's in the dirt. We stayed there for about six months and split up then to get other jobs. We didn't get much gold, about three or four ounces, I suppose.

Then I went back out mustering again, at Skull Springs, Horses Creek, Tarra Tarra, Fig Tree Rockhole, Binbiyanha, Googhenama[2] and Pirrinha[3] Rockhole. All around in that area, Oakover and Davis country. The cattle was very wild. There was no quiet cattle amongst them, all wild stuff. The only way we could handle them when we found a mob is shoot and chase them over on to some stony ridges.

We'd keep away from them making sure they could see us and we could see them. We'd sing and make much noise so they got used to us. We'd take them to the yard. They were

[1]Jack required replacement lumber   [2]Near Gregory's Pool   [3]Pearana Rockhole

as quiet as a lamb then. We put them in the yard, about thirty-six of them, bulls mostly. The next day we branded up and we could drive them anywhere quite easy. It's really quite easy to get wild cattle if you know how to do it. So we got a few more and we put them out on the block of land I had.

We had started a bit of a station and I finished up with five hundred head of cattle. Now and again, we killed some of the cattle. We sold the meat. We were out there until 1937.

By then we had three children, two girls and a boy. We had no motor cars and it was far out. We were always frightened they might get sick. Also it was a dry time. The cattle was alright, they eat the top food, but there was no rain, no feed for the horses. So I had to give it up. In the end I sold all the cattle to different ones. I got rid of all the stock that was there, even the horses.

10

Not for the love of money

A tough old place

I came out to Port Hedland. It was a tough old place, come around about 1937-38. It was very hard. You couldn't get a permanent job in town. Aboriginal men couldn't get a job on the wharf, not for the love of money, too black. We couldn't get a job on the railway line. I was lucky. I worked for Taplin in a garage for about eight months. That used to be straight across from what is now the Commonwealth Bank in Wedge Street. It was a two storey place. It'd been a pub originally. Taplin used the bottom part for the garage and he used to live on the top. He was one of the pilots in the First World War and he came out here from Great Britain, him, Captain Brearley and Charles Kingsford-Smith.

Kingy wasn't alive then, he'd lost his life in 1935, Kingsford-Smith. Him and Keith Anderson I believe, and another chap. They got the fastest plane, Rolls Royce engines I think and they headed for China. They sort of got lost, they landed in

Burma on the beach and one of the wheels got bogged in the mud or sand or something. I don't know what happened to one fella, but Keith Anderson pulled out and Kingy said, "I'll go." So he done the plane up again and he flew to China and that was his last. He got lost, compass went wrong or something, that was in 1935.

Len Taplin had a few trucks. They was pretty rough those days. He had a butcher shop too. Some Aboriginal people worked at the butcher shop and some worked on the trucks carting all the goods out to all the stations, different places, for three quid a week. Most might get a little job for a day or so from somebody and they'd buy flour or bread, tea and sugar. It was very hard.

There wasn't many coloured people here. There was a mob of half-caste people who come down from the North, in the One Mile area, that was our township. There was the Clarkes, some of them still here, the Piantas, Matt Dann and Murphys, two lots of Murphys — two brothers, then there was quite a few of them here, still here now. There was the Hawks, Ellerys, Bill Ellery — he had his family here and the Pedlars. Mort Pedlar, Jack Pedlar and the mother and some kids. Sisters and brothers I suppose, well they were there then.

Times was very very hard for coloured people. We wasn't allowed in town after six o'clock. We had to get out to the One Mile, that was the boundary. We had to stop there until the next morning.

One Mile was opposite Newman on the right hand track, meet Anderson Street, follow that along a bit to the road going up to the hospital, well, that area there, that was One Mile. How we lived there, I don't know.

It was hard to keep a family. The Clarkes had about eight children, two of them got killed in the last war, some of them are still here. The Piantas had five. The old man used to do the laundry work at the hospital for five quid a week.

You couldn't go to school. There was one primary school, I think, in Edgar Street. Next to that was the convent, the Catholics. Well, most of the half-caste people were Catholics. They came from Beagle Bay, all Catholic people. Well, those that wasn't were sent to the primary school, there wasn't too many. Might have been thirty altogether. Times were very very hard.

Now this Citizenship Rights came on, the Exemption Certificate. Well that didn't improve anything very much. I had one for quite a while. Without one you could not go within a hundred yards of an authorised licensed premise. If you did, you'd get jailed, no worries there. You might get a week or you might get a month.

Water was very scarce and wood was very, very scarce. We had to go down and break mangroves to do a bit of cooking. It's not bad wood either. The old mangroves from the mud bay. That's all been scooped out now. It used to be right behind BHP's main buildings down in the creek. Marapikurinha they call it in Aboriginal name. At that time, we had to go fishing pretty often. We used to go every chance we got. We had to, to get a living for our families.

Sometimes we used to come up to Pretty Pool, walk all the way up there, you know, at neap tides. In the ordinary tides, we'd go down at the jetty or over at the mud bay, well they call that Nelson's Point now. We'd catch whatever we could, periwinkles, mudbays, get bags of them along the mangroves, octopus, little ones they are, we used to grab them too.

Often me and old Matt Dann would go out with throw nets and catch whatever we could. Then we'd make Johnny cakes and cook them on the coals of the mangroves and leaves. We cook whatever we could get, fish of any sort and we'd have a good old feed before we'd take a lot home for the children. The good fishing we'd do down on the beach, catching the tides coming in.

Some mornings, me and two old ladies used to go on the beach before sunrise. The tide would start to come in and they would take me for a packhorse with a cordsack. Well, them two old girls were mother Pianta and mother Clarke. They'd do the fishing, I was there pulling them in as quick as possible. I was that full and frightened with the water coming up, up past my knees, nearly to my hips!

I said, "Come on you two, we've got to go home, I can't swim!"

But there was a little deep channel behind us, water was up to my chest. The bag of fish that I had, I was dragging it. The fish were floating along in the water until we got out onto the beach.

I went back prospecting again, back out of Nullagine. There was a fair bit of gold around there, you know, it wasn't hard to get. It was easier there than in Marble Bar. We were prospecting around Boodalarie for about seven months. We wasn't digging everyday, but you know what I mean, we were round there for seven months. I got a bit of gold, thirty ounces, I suppose, altogether. But you couldn't get free gold, all in quartz in rocks. You had to cart it in to the nearest battery at Eastern Creek, sixteen miles away on two pack camels.

It was pretty tough. We had to carry our children in our horse packs. I'd carry one and the wife'd carry the other one and somebody else carried the other one on the other horse in front of them all the time, like that. That's how we lived. It was no use looking for work because if you'd get work, there was no money in it, no money.

When we left there, I went back in closer into the hills, close into Nullagine town. Sometimes I was working in the State Battery to get a few bob, that's at Twenty Mile Sandy out from Nullagine and sometimes I was prospecting for gold at Number Five Head Battery. We'd crush the dirt. You clean it all up and take the silver out of it. You, what they call, re-sort it.[*] The silver comes out of it and leaves the gold in the crucible. You then smelt the gold and pour it into a mould to get a bar. Then you sell it of course.

Oh, we made a decent do of it, you know, it was alright. There was only me, my missus and the three kids. We didn't live like kings or anything but we had plenty to eat. Those days, there was no refrigerators. We had to keep the food as cold as you could, pour it on a wet bag or something like that, you know, to keep it cool. There were charcoal coolers and there was hessian coolers. Well, we didn't have either one of those. We used to wrap up the food and put it in a hole, a damp hollow. We'd wrap the butter or whatever we wanted in a chaff bag, all wet, put it in the hole and cover it up, keep it cool.

In 1939 there was a big cyclone here in Port Hedland. There was no South Hedland those days. It nearly washed Port Hedland away. The creek in front of the Esplanade was running a banker and Pretty Pool was coming down neap, flooding back.

In Wedge Street, anywhere around the Esplanade or the Pier Hotels, there was four foot of water, waves. In Stevens Street, alongside the cemetery, the water came even over there, over the Lock Hospital that used to take all the Aboriginal people. That's the lowest part of the Cooke's Point Ridge. There was like one big sheet of water from Pretty Pool on one side of town to the Esplanade Hotel on the other side. It was a terrible mess.

There used to be a bridge in front of the Esplanade Hotel. It's not there now, that's all filled in and covered up. That was a lake, all water everywhere, salt water. That's why Anderson Street is so crooked today. It used to go around the lake that was there.

[*]Or retort it

The cyclone'd washed the railway line all the way from Port Hedland to Marble Bar. The crossings was all washed away and beds broken up. They couldn't get enough white men, so they put on Aboriginals and that's how it started to come good then.

11

That was the true story

Prospector's memories

I went prospecting properly on my own after. By that time we had four children. I was at Nullagine digging gold, putting it through crushings. I put two crushings, a hundred tonne a year. We'd get about fifty, sixty ounces of gold for the year.

The price of gold was nine pound an ounce at that time. I didn't have a mate. I had a motor car. I'd dry-blow around Cookes Creek and Mosquito Creek and I done alright. I had no boss.

One fella got shot there. He's supposed to have been a German. So they said. He was camped there, dry-blowing, shaking the dry-blower for golds. Sorenson, his name was. The blackfellas were travelling through and he was camped in his boughshed not far from the government well, only about a hundred yards away. He woke up. He could hear this noise.

So he got up and had a look. He seen a mob of blackfellas at the well pulling water and he went to his humpy and picked up a forty-four rifle. He fired a shot and split the windless barrel.

There's a deep creek not far from there, about ten feet away, Mosquito Creek. They ran down along that. He never caught them. They didn't have a drink of water, so they went on to Eight Mile, a claypan, where there was water. It's dirty and all that sorta thing, but they had to have something. Later, they went on to Nullagine River and up to Nullagine.

There was nothing mentioned about him getting killed then, but about two or three months later, someone said to somebody, "Anybody seen old Sorenson about? He hasn't been around here and hasn't been seen going to Nullagine to get tucker or anything."

So they went looking for him. They searched for him but they couldn't find him. They found his camp. When he was shot, he was carried below Lower Mosquito and put on the top of a hill, the Black Range and covered over with a lot of rocks. The police asked different blackfellas.

"No, we never see 'um, we never see 'um."

There was a chap called Tom Byas, the police asked him, "Have you seen old Sorenson about?"

"No."

"Well, we asked different blackfellas and they don't know anything about it. We'll give you some whisky. Go out there where there is a mob and get them half drunk. They might let it out then."

Sure enough, they did. Oh yeah, they had a row amongst themselves, you know.

"Oh yes, I'm kill 'em whitefella not long ago."

"Don't pull one on me." So on.

So any rate, the police went up. They were listening in behind the bushes at night-time. So they went up, caught them and put them in jail, but they caught the wrong ones! The one that had killed him never got touched!

So anyway, they caught another chap, Paddy, who was working for a bloke called Bill Smith on horse drays. They caught him and another fella named Pincher. They jailed them two. Both got trialled and all the rest of it, and they were sent away down to the settlement. They got fifteen years.

Paddy went in to the Sergeant he was working for at Kalgoorlie. He went up to him, "Well Sergeant, I done my time, I done my fifteen years. What about let me go home now? Put me on the train and tell Neville I've finished."

"Alright Paddy, but you gotta go and see Neville."

He went to see him and Neville said, "Oh, I don't think you should go Paddy, better stop here."

"Oh, I must go Mr Neville, I must go! Well, I want some clothes too."

"Oh well, alright, I'll give you a note and you take it to Boan Brothers and get what clothes you want."

So that was it. He got his fare. The boat was ready to leave the wharf at Fremantle. He had to catch the train to there. He found out the biggest suitcase he could find and filled it up with a lot of things. He got on the train, went down on the wharf and caught the ship back to Port Hedland.

The first place he went to when he got back to Port Hedland, was the police station. He told them his name and what he wanted. A fare back to Marble Bar.

"Oh well," Sergeant said, "Alright then, Wednesday the train leaves here. You go to Marble Bar, I give you a ticket."

He became a police tracker afterwards in Marble Bar. He was working for the police there until 1956 I think it was and when he left, he went out to Moolyella getting tin. He died somewhere around about 1973. That was the true story. He told it to me himself. He'd never killed Sorenson at all but he got the blame.

No one could make out how Paddy Darby got mixed up in it, you know. He wasn't with them blackfellas at all. The man that killed Sorenson was Jackie Bunandi. Yeah,

Bunandi, he died over at Yandeyarra or at Warralong in 1982 or might be 1983.

Of course there was a few more mixed up in it, but they all got out. These other two did the time for nothing. They had to take the blame for somebody else. The other fella, Pincher, he died in Nullagine. He got the blame too for nothing, like with Paddy at the Moore River Settlement.

These two old fellas, they come to Nullagine and that's where I got this information from about the Great Fingall in Day Dawn, like how it was worked and all that sorta thing. They had a horse down there underground, pulling the trolley. Well, it contained ten ounces in a tonne. They took two tonne in a dray, horse dray about twenty-five miles to the nearest battery and they treated it. They got five ounces of gold out of it, and the concentrates, they put that in the four hundred gallon square tank. There was somewhere around about sixty percent of copper and still five ounces per tonne in the copper. They couldn't get it out.

So one fella said, "Well, I don't know much about copper, but for gold, we can go over to the Conglomerates." So they put this dirt through the Conglomerates and when it was cleaned up, they found another diamond in the corner of the box. It was hard work to break it up, but they got it and they found out it was worth seventy-five quid. There has been a few diamonds found since, but only small ones about the size of a match head.

Another battery, about twenty miles out of Nullagine, they called it McPhee's, it was pretty good. They shifted the battery back to Nullagine again and done a few more crushings there from different places, from Barton and Castlemaine. Well at Castlemaine, one tonne of dirt produced about seventy-five ounces of gold or something like that.

Billy Baker and some others carted some gold. They had two horse drays, they carted the stone from Boodalyerri across to Yandicoogina. There was a battery there. They crushed that stone there. It wasn't quite good enough, not what they'd expected, you know. The gold was a little bit poor, it was only seven thousand carats, so they didn't do anymore there and it's still there. They went prospecting the other way.

Somewhere else, other two fellas, Archie Swan, Billy Moxon — Jack Kennedy, he was a windmill man on Warrawagine Station and he found and opened a lead mine, called Ragged Hills. He got Archie Swan and Billy Moxon in with him as partners — they used to break the lead up, put it in forty-four gallon drums and cart it the best way they could into Coongan Siding for the railway to pick up. But the price of lead was pretty poor, so they gave it up.

Archie Swan and Billy Moxon, they had camels, mostly pack camels and a riding camel. They went on their own again out to the Twenty Ounce Gully, near Mt Edgar Station. Mt Edgar Station was owned by Lionel Taylor and Fred Devonport. Anyhow, they got a bit of luck. They found a fair bit of gold in one of the places there, a place they call Bullgarina. They made quite a bit of money out of it. I think all the gold was in four or five kerosene tins, a dab, what you call a dab, very rich dirt, only a bit of quartz and a lot of gold. They crushed thirty tonne. I don't know how much gold they got, but it was terribly rich. Archie Swan, after he got all this money his share of the money, he went over east to Victoria somewhere. He died over there. Billy Moxon remained at the Twenty Ounce and didn't spend his money. He stayed there.

Later on in years, Fred Green went over the Twenty Ounce from Talga Talga and saw old Billy Moxon there, nearly dead. He couldn't walk about or get a drop of water. So Fred picked him up and took him to Marble Bar to hospital. He was an old man. He didn't get over it properly. He died two weeks later. That year was 1936.

...you can have this. You can have
Mrs Palmer and her five daughters.
These five daughters here

We used to cart wool with camel wagons
from the Talga and Bonney Downs
into the Coongan Sidings...

That was a government well. That was the best water. The McKenna family

Mick Blair yandying for tin, standing, Paddy Blair sitting. The strike, Moolyella

Paddling tin, Moolyella 1904

The Thompsons, first family in Marble Bar.
Standing L-R: Alf, Joe Don, Sandy
Sitting L-R: Rod, Mrs Thompson, Bill
On ground: Jack

Port hedland...dropped a few bombs in the water near the harbour there

...Prince Gibson. He knows the road out here. Tell him to bring out a tyre

Some Pilbara mine workings

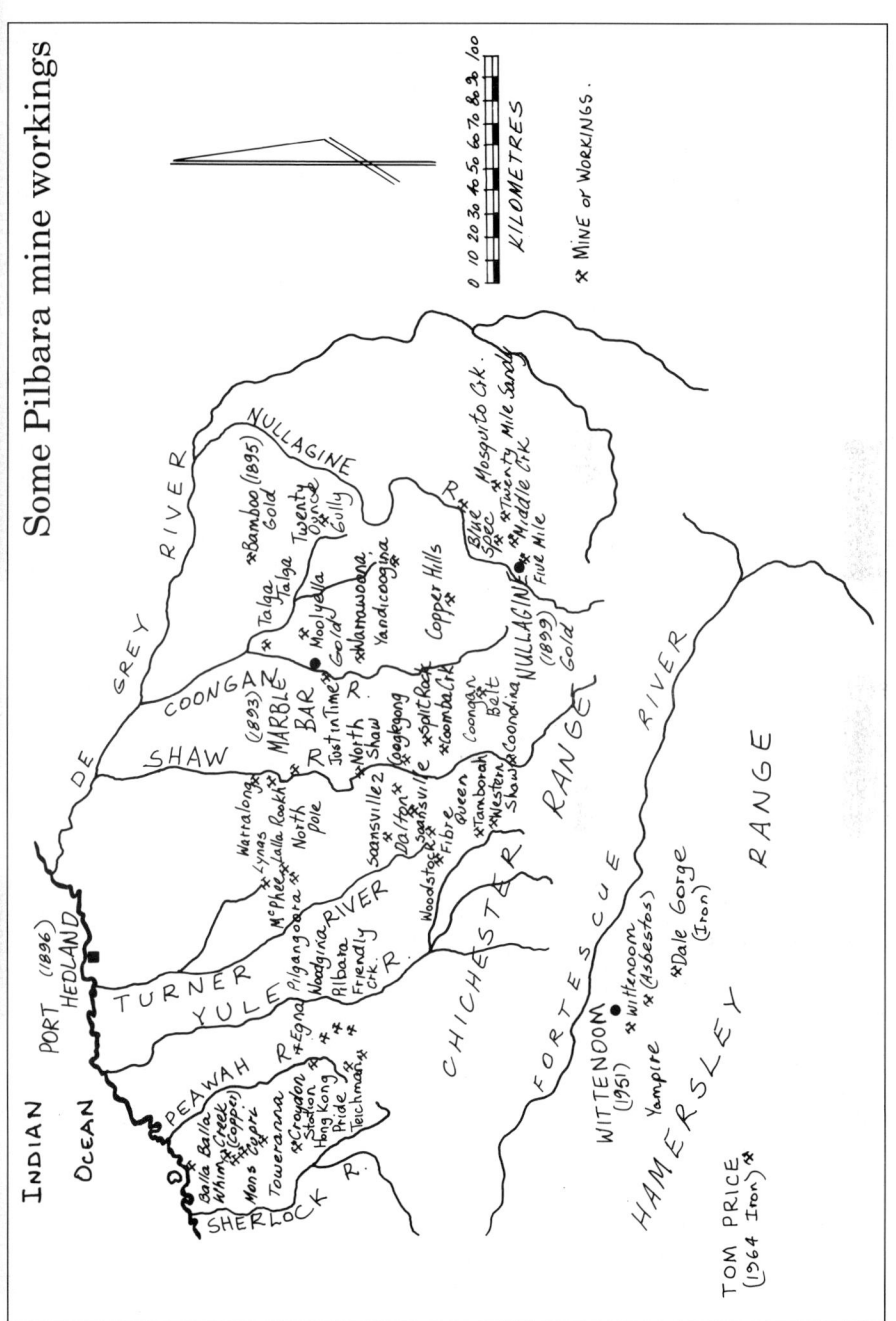

KILOMETRES

0 10 20 30 40 50 60 70 80 90 100

✗ MINE or WORKINGS.

INDIAN OCEAN

PORT HEDLAND (1896)

GREY RIVER

DE GREY

NULLAGINE RIVER

✗ Bamboo (1895) Gold
✗ Talga Talga
Twenty Ounce Gully
✗ Moolyella Gold
✗ Warrawoona
Yandicoogina
Copper Hills ✗
✗ Blue Spec
Mosquito Ck. ✗
✗ Twenty Mile Sandy
✗ Middle Ck.
Five Mile ●

COONGAN

SHAW

MARBLE BAR (1893) ●
R. Just in Time Gold
North Shaw R.
✗ Coogegong
✗ Split Rock
✗ Coomba Ck.
Coongan Belt
NULLAGINE (1899) Gold
Coondina

✗ Watralonga
✗ Lynas
✗ McPhee ✗ Jalla Rockh ✗
North Pole
✗ Soansville 2
✗ Dalton ✗
Soansville
Fibre Queen
✗ Tamborah
✗ Western Shaw

CHICHESTER RANGE

FORTESCUE RIVER

TURNER

YULE RIVER

✗ Egina Pilgangoora ✗
✗ Woodgina R.
✗ Pilbara
Friendly Ck.
Woodstock ✗

PEAWAH

✗ Balla Balla
✗ Whim Creek (Copper)
Mons Cupri ✗
✗ Towerranna
✗ Croydon Station
✗ Hong Kong
Pride R.
✗ Teichmann
✗

SHERLOCK R.

WITTENOOM (1951) ●
✗ Wittenoom
✗ Yampire (Asbestos)
✗ Dale Gorge (Iron)

HAMERSLEY RANGE

TOM PRICE (1964 Iron) ✗

Warralong Station...Frank Welsh was the manager there

A lot of people was getting robbed and all that sorta thing, you know. It was very funny, but when you come to think of it, it was terrible. Especially the full-blooded Aboriginals who didn't know anything very much, they'd get robbed hand over fist.

The gold might be worth a hundred quid for an ounce of gold. You might get a hundred quid, but they'd only get a bag of flour or something. Might be a little bit of tea or sugar. It's hard to believe, but it is right. Oh, it was terrible up there. White people robbing each other too, not only white people robbing Aboriginal people.

I've been robbed but not by gold, by a goldmine, yes. See, I found a goldmine, well it turned into a mine after. I took crushings out of it, it was alright. The lease was pegged in the name of this mate of mine, not mine. We agreed I should get half of every-thing that come out of it! Well, this fella he went away and sold it, sold the show, the gold patch. I got nothing.

See, things like that, very cunning, it was a whitefella. This was at Mountain Maid Goldmine, Twenty Mile Sandy out from Nullagine town in 1938.

An old chap named Jimmy Drake was going from Eastern Creek into Nullagine town one day. It's fifty-six miles in from Eastern Creek to Nullagine. So, I asked him could I come in with him. He had a Dodge utility.

When we got to Doherty's Reward Goldmine, as we were going along the road, there's blackfellas there camped. They threw a boomerang across the road. Jimmy Drake pulled up.

He knew the blackfellas too, old Jimmy.

He said, "Yes, what you want Jimmy?"

"Oh, you takem me Nullagine, Five Mile?"

"Alright, hop on then."

Jimmy said, "Alright, I get my boomerang."

"Oh?" the other old fella, Jimmy Drake, said, "Oh, I can't wait that long, you come another time."

So we went in and next morning, that old fella that threw the boomerang, he was in Five Mile too. The bloke that owned the store there, Paddy Conway said to Jimmy, the blackfella, "What for you never come with Jimmy Drake yesterday?"

"Oh," Jimmy the blackfella said, "Jimmy Drake too much a hurry up, oh yeah, too much a hurry up."

"Oh? How much gold you got Jimmy?" Conway asked.

"One nugget, flat big piece."

Yeah, about twelve ounces I suppose. It looked like that, about twelve. Anyway, he puts it on the counter and ties it in a handkerchief.

The shopkeeper said, "Oh, you got 'em good one."

Paddy Conway wouldn't say. He wouldn't give him an idea if there was ten or twelve or one ounce even. He wouldn't say that. He's cunning too, but the poor old blackfella, he didn't know how much it was.

Paddy Conway, the storekeeper, he wanted that gold, you know, and he wanted to give only a little bit for it, not much. So he said to Jimmy, "What you want 'em Jimmy?" Jimmy said, "I want 'em dobago, matchies, sugar, tea, plauer."

That's tobacco, matches, sugar, tea and flour.

Paddy Conway said, "That's gonna cost you a hundred pounds."

It was only worth about eight quid, I suppose, eight pound, not a hundred pounds but he charged him a hundred pounds.

"Anything you want more?"

"Yeah, I want a tin meat."

"Anything else?"

"Yeah, tardin." Sardines.

Paddy kept the tally, you know, so he knew when he gave him enough. He charged heavy to get that stuff, that gold, quicker. "Now anything else Jimmy?"

"Yeah, tana, dausa." Shirt and trousers.

"Yeah Jimmy, anything else?"

"Yeah, djina djina. Mummy want 'em djina djina."

Dress: djina djina.

"Anything else Jimmy?"

"Aah yes. Two pikinini want 'em djina djina too." Two little girls, daughters of his, they want dresses too.

"Yeah, anything else Jimmy?"

"Yes, this one two men here, he want 'em tana and dausa." Two sons of his, they're only little fellas, but they want shirts and trousers.

"Oh, alright Jimmy. You can't get much more Jimmy, the gold is just about sold out!"

He was robbing the poor soul, robbing him, you know!

"Oh yeah, anything else you want 'em?"

"Yes, aahm, me want 'em bruit." Fruit, tin fruit.

"How many?"

"Six altogether."

"Oh well, I think you're in debt to me now Jimmy. You can't have anymore."

"Me get 'em more gold," he said. I get some more gold.

He already had it in another bag, but in small lumps, you know. He'd pick them out, a little bit at a time. That big one still got plenty, but the storekeeper was robbing him, charging three times more than what it was worth, sometimes five times more than what it was worth! Oh, a lot of that went on up there.

"Yes, well aahm, how much you want 'em now? What do you want 'em now?"

Conway had seen the gold, the new lot come in.

"Oh, what do you want 'em now?"

"I want 'em pipe." A pipe to smoke.

"Yes, you know, pipe very dear!" Paddy Conway said to him. "Pipe very dear, cost about thirty quid."

That's worth about three bob I suppose, that's at that time, but he charged him thirty quid for it, robber!

"Yes aahm, which way you camp now Jimmy?"

"Kukal Creek."

Cookes Creek he mean to say, but he said Kukal Creek.

"Oh, now how you gonna go back there?" Paddy asked Jimmy.

"I don't know."

"I'll take you out for a hundred quid. "

It was only about twenty mile out.

"Yeah ulrait." Alright.

"But, you'll owe me about hundred and fifty. You'll have to get some more gold."

"Oh, get 'em more gold."

He asked his woman to give him a bit more, another three or four more pieces.

"You still owe me a lot more though, that's not enough."

"No, no more got 'em anymore here, we finish now gold."

"Yeah, well you still owe me about a hundred now."

Paddy Conway took him out to Cookes Creek, left him out there and they had to dig up more gold. They had to take it in otherwise they wouldn't get anymore tucker, no credit. Conway wouldn't give him any credit. The stuff that Jimmy had bought was only worth about a hundred quid, mightn't even have been that ! The price that Conway would have got was somewhere about four thousand! Oh, robber, he was!

Another time, another blackfella, Jacky Aspro, they called him, came into Paddy Conway's shop.

"Yeah, Jackie what do you want?"

"Oh, want 'em tucker." Food.

"Yes, you got 'em gold?"

"Yes, I got 'em gold."

There was a lot of gold those days up there, you know, easy got, loose gold, 'luvial.

"Yes, I got 'em gold."

"Yeah, what do you want 'em?"

"I want some aah, dobago, matchies." Tobacco and matches.

"And five altogether aspro." Five packets of Aspro, aspirins. That was good stuff too, medicine, but he was overdoing it, you know. Instead of havin' one or two, he'd have about half-a-dozen. A packet didn't last that long.

So Conway gave him that, but he still had a few more bob of that gold. Paddy Conway didn't want to let that gold go. He started to push stuff over on to him.

"What about you buy 'em bicycle now?"

"Yes, ulrait." Alright.

But, he couldn't ride the blooming thing, only just push it! So, he sold him that for a hundred quid. The bike was only worth about twelve quid those days, sometimes twenty-five quid. The BSAs, they were real good bikes, I had one myself.

"Yes aah, ulrait, I buy 'em."

So, he took it half a mile and give it away to somebody else, because he couldn't ride it. It was pushed onto him sort of business, so that Paddy Conway could get all the gold.

"Yeah, anything else you want 'em?"

"Aah, I got 'em jilaman out there, I got no kadridj." Jilaman means gun, he had one out the camp, but he had no cartridges for it.

"Oh yeah, you got a licence for jilaman?"

"Blackfella can't buy 'em licence, he's a poor fella."

"Oh well, you gotta have a licence, I can't give you cartridges if you got no licence, but I'll sneak it around to you."

"Ulrait." Alright.

So he gave him a packet of cartridges.

One time, Aspro Jack goes out, just about sundown, and he pushed a rock out of the road and it was half gold. There was seventy-five ounces of gold on it, when they dollied it up! Old Frank Paul weighed it. He had seventy-five ounces of this specimen amongst the stone. Aspro Jacky, when he found it, sold it to another blackfella called Paddy Luva, gave it to him.

Anyhow, Paddy Luva goes in with this seventy-five ounces and takes it to Conway.

"Oh, you got 'em gold?"

"Yes," he said, "It's seventy-five ounces."

"Now, who give you that, who told you that?"

"Oh, Frank Paul."

"Yeah? How he know?"

"Oh, he got 'em scale."

"Oh yeah? What for you takem there? This is the place you oughta be bring 'em here. I weigh 'em properly."

"Oh, don't matter now, I been takem there," he said.

"Oh yeah, well aah, it's worth a lot of money. I suppose you want a lot a things too?"

"Yes, five bag flour."

"Yes, what else?"

"One chide piggy-piggy." One side of ham, bacon.

"Yes, what else you want?"

"Oh, I wantem one case meat."

"Yes, anything else?"

"Bruit, I wantem bruit." Fruit, tins of fruit.

"Yeah."

"And dobago, matchies, bundle." A bundle of tobacco and matches.

"Well, you just about...you got a lot of stuff, Paddy, anything else?"

"Yes, I wantem motor car, truck."

"Oh well, there's one over there under the tree over there, but he only got three wheels."

"Yeah?"

"Yes."

"How much?"

"Oh," he said, "lotta money, but he only got three wheels. You'll have to go and get a wheel somewhere."

It was an old Reo, I know the bus. Old Reo truck, but someone had pinched one of the wheels off it. The truck wasn't like these good ones, you know. It had to be fixed up and that.

So, Paddy Luva said, "He won't, he won't go that wheel in there." He said, "He no good."

"Oh well, I'll get Bill Burton, the mechanic, to try to fix it for you."

"Yeah, ulrait." Alright.

He got the wheel, they had to send away to Perth and get one. Of course Paddy Luva was charged…a thousand quid! So, he had two now. The storekeeper and this mechanic bloke, he was charging him twenty-five pound an hour.

Conway said, "Cost lotta money to work on these Paddy, twenty-five pound an hour."

"Yeah?"

"Yeah, that wheel already cost you a thousand quid from Perth. I had to write a letter and send it down to United Motors — and get it up here by train as far as Meekatharra and from there on Overland Mail in the truck to Nullagine. That cost a thousand dollars, you know Paddy?"

"Yeah?"

"Yeah."

Oh, it fitted alright, he got the right wheel fitted alright.

Well, they found out when they put the water in the radiator that it went right through. There was a big hole in the bottom tank.

"He no good that radiator, that won't hold 'em water," Paddy Luva said.

"What's wrong with it?"

"We fill 'em up here water, he go right through."

"Oh yes? Oh well, we put a bit of cement on it," the mechanic said.

"Yes ulrait."

See, the tank, it was on the chassis like that. Well, it was leaking out on the joint, you know the bottom tank onto the core, the radiator core. It was all just coming away sort of business. The mechanic said, "We put some cement on it."

"Yes ulrait."

He put that on it. The water come up then to the edge of the cement.

"Oh," he said.

"Put on some more cement."

It went up a bit further. Water still came up to the end of the cement and come out again, you see it still leaked.

"Oh, he no good, he still leaking."

"Oh, we'll put some more cement on it."

In the finish, the front of the radiator was all cement! It would only go as far as from here to the shop I suppose. It'd be boiling, get no air through the holes!

"He no good, no buy 'em no more. A fireplace!"

"Yeah?"

"Yeah."

"Well, I can get you another radiator, might cost you two thousand quid."

"Yeah?"

"Yeah, I'll have to get it up from Perth. See, it's a lot of work getting it up here. I've got to write a letter about the radiator to the United Motors."

It was a second hand one too, but they told him it was a new one. "So, we get it up by rail to Meekatharra and by Overland Mail from Nullagine. It'll cost you just two thousand, might cost you little bit more."

Poor buggar! Oh, a lot of that was going on there. Even white people, they were beating one another.

Old Billy Lynas, old white chap, I know him well. He came to Nullagine. He had a bit of luck. He found a reef of gold, pretty rich too. He had a sugar bag full of specimens off the reef. You know, the old seventy-five pound sugar bag, you don't see them now. That was nearly full of these specimens.

Old Billy Lynas liked plenty of grog too, you know, alcohol. Another whitefella come along, they were talking about it.

"How you going Billy? "

"Oh," he said, "Good."

He went out with the bag and showed it to him and said, "Look what I got here in this bag."

"Oh geez, they're lovely aren't they? Nearly all gold, no stone in 'em."

"Yeah."

They was talking there for a little while. Then, this fella, he was a business bloke, went to town, Nullagine, and there's three other business blokes there. Anyhow, they got talking about Billy Lynas's good find. So one fella said, "I'll tell you what we'll do. We'll take him out a bag of grog and another empty bag. We'll fill it up with stones." So, they took it out. They did that, the four of them. They gets out there. Billy was in his camp.

"G'day Billy, g'day, how are you feeling?"

"Oh beautiful, beautiful."

"Oh good, yes. Did you have any luck?"

"Oh yes. Look at all the gold I got in this bag, these specimens."

"Oh, by gee! They're nice aren't they, Billy? Well, look Billy, we brought you out some drink. We brought three or four different sorts, we don't know which ones you like, but you can have the lot of them."

There was beer, whisky, brandy, rum and wine. So they sat down and old Billy opened a bottle of beer and getting that into him. Then somebody said, "Have a drink of whisky with me."

The other bloke, he was cunning too. Instead of drinking it, he was just putting it to his mouth and chucking it away. Old Billy, he'd drink that and beer and whisky on top of that, soon it knocked him over. They watching all this, that's all they were doing. Trying to get him drunk to put him to sleep so they could take this good bag of gold away and put this one with no gold at all in it.

That's what they did. They got a hundred and sixty ounces of gold, after they took the rock out of it. The four of them shared it amongst each other. I don't know what they got. It was nine pound an ounce. You can just imagine, they got a good bit of money each out of it. Oh yeah, they was pretty crook those fellas at that time.

Billy was dead to the world, drunk, flat out. When he woke up, he was a sick man and he started looking around. He was gonna have some more grog, it was there. He didn't take much notice of this bag of gold, you know what I mean, he thought that was alright. He didn't know any better for a long time. He had a big heap of stones crushed there from the battery, big heap.

Billy McKinnon, he went prospecting up around the Marble Bar area and he found a place they call Just in Time. There was some other shows worked there but not big, you know. They were only taking the good stuff out and crushing it at Marble Bar State Battery. Billy McKinnon found this big, good reef. It wasn't rich, but there was plenty of it. I worked there, I worked down at three hundred foot level. They had lifts there imported from Europe but the water beat them there, too much water. They couldn't keep up. He got thirty thousand for it. So, he went to Nullagine and pegged the Conglomerate.

He thought he was going to make a fortune, but he didn't. He put up a house, bought some machinery and he went broke. He still had a truck left and some tools, he didn't sell them. He said to me one day, he said, "I wonder could you put us onto something Jack?"

"Oh well," I said, "I can help you, I don't know about putting you onto anything good. Course my kids are grown up and they have to go to school. I got notice from the Child Welfare, you know, but while I'm waiting, I'll give you a hand."

So we went truck driving, I went truck driving for him, me and an old fella called Con O'Brien. We were getting eight weights of gold a day. Well, that paid us. We didn't have to mine it, we just picked up the dry-blowing dumps, you know. Then I left him. I had to go for the sake of the children.

Old Bill carried on and on and on, and he found a pipe of diamonds. But too small, if you understand, it was just one pipe going down at the Conglomerate. So his wife went away to Cottesloe with the family, barring the boy of course. He stayed with Bill. Then he had a good look around but he couldn't find nothing any good.

They never came home

Turbulent times

It was 1941 and I had to come down and bring the children to school. There was two of them fit for school. That was Marie and Johnny, the two biggest ones. There's a lot of kids about then. Some at the Comet Goldmine and some all around about the place. There must have been fifty, sixty kids. The primary school'd just started to open up then.

A chap named Jack Hutchinson, he started the school going. He was the first teacher. When we were kids, there was no school there. The first school house was put up by Charlie Bayman. That was the same man who put up the Port Hedland Post Office in 1914, I think it was.

I worked on the Road Board for a while then, the Marble Bar Road Board. I got a job truck driving for the Road Board, carting dirt and everything, me and Doug Francis...that's the boss. He was on the grader. There was the boss, me and another fella on the truck, Barkley Elleridge. We went on that for quite a while, might be eight, nine months. It was all hard work. There was no machinery those days. Our machines were wheelbarrows, picks and shovels, I'd only get seven quid a week, fourteen pound a fortnight. It wasn't very much to keep your wife and four children. So I went and worked on the Comet.

The Comet Mine was found by an Aboriginal chap, old Ginger. Two old prospectors had been working that gully for a long time with a dry-blower, but they couldn't make out where the gold was coming from. So this Aboriginal fella, old Ginger, he walked up the creek with a gun to get a kangaroo. When he went up there, he seen the kangaroo. He shot him and wounded him and it climbed up the hill. Old Ginger followed the kangaroo and it dropped not far from where this gold was sticking out. You could see it sticking out from the quartz, funny sorta quartz it was...and so, alright, he went back and told them.

They said, "Alright Ginger, we'll pay you for it. We'll give you a lot of money for that."

So anyway, they went up and had a look, he showed them where it was. They said, "Alright, we'll go to town."

They had to go in to the Mines Department to peg it out, and they also went over to the bank and the store. In the store, they asked Albert Hansen, the storekeeper, to give Ginger a bag of flour and a little bit of tea, sugar and a bit of tobacco and he was paid.

Right, so they went and worked it, they crushed twenty tonne and made a fortune out of it! It went fifteen ounces with a tonne. So they thought they were too old to go working any depths.

Claude De Bernales, he had a show with a mob of men working it, a place they call Little Wonder. So De Bernales went and bought the Comet for forty thousand off them. They threw up the Little Wonder, it wasn't so good, and they shifted everything to Comet. Poor old Ginger, all he got was a bag of flour and a little bit of tea and sugar and they got thousands out of it!

It was very very good at the Comet, but it was underground. I was down at two hundred foot level, but I had to keep my family going. My fifth child, Doreen was born by then.

Oh well, at that time, the Jap war'd started, there was hardly anybody in town. The Japs started to bomb Port Hedland and dropped a few bombs in the water near the harbour there. They came at sunrise, along the beach with planes, and travelled very low.

I'd wanted to join the VDC, the Voluntary Defence Call,* but my eyes wasn't good enough to go to the Army. There was quite a lot of Aboriginal people who went from here to Burma and Timor. Some of them are here now but some never came back. There was five half-caste people who went from here. That was Manny Lockyer, Arnold Lockyer, Eric Lockyer, Tommy Murphy and Jimmy Clarke. Two of them, two of the brothers never came back, that's Arnold and Eric. They never returned, they never came home. Also Tommy Gray, he was head stockman on Anna Plains, when he joined up.

There was the army airport, the American's main base at Corunna Downs. It's just out from Marble Bar, twenty-four miles out. Oh, they used to have great big bombers there!

When we used to go on shift at four o'clock, they'd start. You'd see them coming over in waves, big bombers and fighters too, but bombers mainly. Mitchells and...oh I forget what the names of the planes was.

They used to go over to Timor from there. They'd work all night and come back in the morning with shattered tails, wobbling about and half broken down. They just managed to get home, some of them. That was in somewhere around about 1943.

*Volunteer Defence Corps

I got a touch of Pyorrhoea in the gums, then. Your gums swell up. You don't have a toothache or anything but if you bite anything hard, it starts to bleed. I went to the doctor, Dr Dicks and he said, "Hmm, you'll have to get all your teeth pulled out. Well, I can't do anything for you because there's no dentist here. You got to have a dentist to do that Jack, so I'll order you to Perth."

I said, "Alright."

I went to Dr Hogan in North Fremantle and he said, "Well, you'll have to get a dentist and I'll be the doctor."

So I went to the Gosnells Dentist, Peter Bennett his name was. They couldn't pull them all out at once. They pulled half out and the doctor said, "We'll have to stop otherwise all the blood might choke him."

So I had a fortnight off and then he pulled the rest out. Thirty-two teeth he pulled out.

In between getting my teeth out, I got a job at the Colonial Sugar Refinery in Fremantle. It was a good job, very good pay but sticky, very sticky working sugar molasses, some as hard as rock. You had to break it with a big long mallet.

I seen Elma while I was down there. I'd found out where she lived from her brother Des Corboy. I was working for him on the Barton Mine and he told me where they lived, number of the house in West Leederville. So when I went down, I went to them and I stayed most of the day with them, with Elma and the mother and the stepfather, old Maurice McKenna, I suppose he'd be a stepfather and old Frank Hall. That's the last I seen Elma. I never seen her no more after that. They were good people, real good.

Anyway I worked at the Colonial Sugar Refinery for about eleven months and I had to leave then because we had trouble finding a home to stay in. We was staying with friends all the time. It was hard. We had six children by then.

My old friend, Wally Dowling, who'd worked with me for Harry Farber many years ago, when we were young, you know, when he grew up, got old enough, he got a plant of horses of his own and got a mob of cattle and brought them across on the Canning Stock Route, round to Wiluna. I don't know what year that was, I think it's somewhere around about 1938, I'm not sure.

Then when four wheel drives came in, Landrovers, somewhere around about 1942-43, they had to get a person that knew the bush country and that was Wally Dowling. They had four Landrovers, one was full of fuel, another one was full of water, you know drums of water and another one with all their swags and blankets and all that sorta thing and another one full of food.

They went across from Windy Springs, North of Wiluna as far as I can make out, straight across the desert to Billiluna, that's way up in the Kimberley. They were the first four wheel drives that came out, the Landrovers.

The Toyota didn't come out here until about 1974. They wasn't as good as the ones today. They was the first lot that came up. Of course, there might've been plenty over east and other places, but I'm talking about the Pilbara. They wasn't so good.

13

You took what you could get

Struggling for a living

When Hitler threw his towel in, when President Roosevelt died and President Truman took over the Presidency of America and when John Curtin of Australia was the Prime Minister, I was working at Mt Magnet, Hill Fifty Goldmine. That's in 1945. I was there for about eleven months on that job, it was pretty good. I nearly got killed two or three times underground. Three other people got killed, not far from me, but I didn't, I escaped. Then I bought a car, a truck and drove back to Marble Bar to return to my old job at the Comet Goldmine.

We had to apply for our Citizenship Rights. Before that we had permits, but they changed it to Citizenship Rights. Before, we wasn't allowed to own anything. We wasn't allowed to own, I don't know about a house, but any large stock, station or so, wasn't allowed to own one. Wasn't allowed to do any droving or be in charge of anything. We was just classed as, oh well, you might as well say animals, you know, that way. So after we got the Citizenship Rights, we was equal, equal to any white person. Even foreigners from other countries had to apply for citizenship rights.

The Comet was a good mine. It was going three ounces a tonne, but they couldn't treat the concentrates. It wasn't clean rock — with tantalite — they couldn't clean it. So De Bernales gave it up and left old Stuart Stubbs there. In the finish, he got the lot. I think he's still there.

At one time, there was quite a lot of people working there. There must've been three shifts, ten in every shift, like in the mine I'm talking about. Then there was eight or nine in the plant working. There's a chimney stack there, it's two hundred and fifty foot high and eight foot across, very big. That was to cook the mineral, the concentrates, to get the gold out of it.

Later, Stubbsy went on treating the sand, cyanide. I think that's cut out now, it's finished with, but he's just still sitting there waiting for some muggins to come along with plenty of money. I think he wants a million for it, so they say, I don't know.

They took up Copper, old Stubbsy, what they call the Copper Hill. That's out between Marble Bar and Nullagine. He done alright there when the copper boom was on, same as this asbestos, you know. But they had to knock it off, it killed people. It's dangerous, it gets in your skin, into your body. I've never worked with them, I never worked copper or asbestos. You've only got to get a whiff of it. It's killed a lot of my friends! The doctors have got no cure for it and that was the end of that.

Anyway, work at the Comet started to wind down. People started to go off, getting put off and all sorts of things. We was looking for jobs and things like that. I went working for a carpenter. That was in Marble Bar police station, post office, courthouse, everything all in one building. Well we took all the roof off and had to put new girders in, rafters and girders, purlins and everything, new iron, all on that roof. That was in 1946. Then the school, we had to put a new one up. The old one was finished, buggered. So we done the school, then that work cut out too.

We couldn't leave Marble Bar because there was the school for the children, but we fathers used to go out and leave the family there in town.

I went out on the tin. The tin price started to go up a bit, about seven and six a pound we got for it. We'd be dry-blowing or doing anything at all to get a few bob for a living to keep our families going. We stopped at that for a long time. There was quite a mob of us.

Well one fella, he was there prospecting for tin. "Who's that old bloke over there?"

"Oh, he looks like an old fossicker."

Well, he's a prospector. Like West Australians would say, "That's a prospector." South Australians would say, "That's a fossicker."

See what I mean? Like the South Australian, he's a Crow Eater and the West Australian, he's a Sandgroper.

Anyway, that young fella went across for a holiday to England from South Australia. When he got over there, he met up with a girl and got engaged. He didn't have time to get married over there. So he came home and they got married in South Australia. Her mother was still over there. Six months later, she came across to Perth and got on the train, the Transcontinental for South Australia.

Well, anyway she gets in the same carriages with these three or four other old people. When they were going across the Nullarbor Plains, a lot of kangaroos hopping about everywhere, this old lady'd never seen a kangaroo before, and she said to these old four, "What are those things hopping over there?"

One of the old fellas said, "Oh, that's the dinkum, they are the real dinkum Australians."

"Oh, are they? My daughter's married to one of them!"

I think he came from Oodnadatta, the township in South Australia. The railway then went from there to Darwin through to Alice Springs. Well, this boy and this girl who got married, they took the old lady up to Darwin in this train. When they got somewhere past Alice Springs, they seen a lot of wild blackfellas standing by the railway line. They were, you know, just looking. They didn't know what a train was. They're all painted up and she covered herself up. She didn't want the blackfellas to see her, this old lady from England. They went to Darwin. Don't know where they went from there. That was the end of the story about this old lady.

We might get jobs now and again, but it wasn't much good. There was hardly any pay, you understand, only seven quid a week, well that wouldn't keep too much. It wouldn't keep a family going.

They were patchy jobs. You'd get a job wherever you'd get one. You'd try anything to get that tucker. It wasn't easy. That's when Don McLeod lead all the blackfellas on strike. He got four leaders. Clancy McKenna, Jacob Oberdoo, Dooley Bin Bin and also Snowy Judmai. They all went on strike and they been that way ever since.

I was talking to Don McLeod one day. He had a mob out prospecting everywhere, wherever they wanted to go look for gold or whatever they could get, you know. They were on strike. So I said to Don that day, "Well," I said, "I can't tell you where the gold is, but I can tell you where it was got," and that sort of thing, "But what about wolfram?"

"Yeah, well that might be alright."

"I can tell you where it's new."

I said to him, "You can go and open that up and see what it's like, if it's lucky."

The price of wolfram was way up high, you know. They got terrible lot of it, they must've made thousands out of it.

When they got a few thousand, that was in Cookes Creek out from Nullagine, they came to Marble Bar and they done a bit of prospecting there, some of them. Some of them went out to Yandeyarra Station.

That was Don McLeod and Ernie Mitchell. They were there together for a while, the whole mob, you know, big mob. Some out at Mt Frisco chasing tin and tantalite. McLeod and Mitchell couldn't agree with each other. McLeod said, "Oh well, you can keep Yandeyarra and I'll go and buy Strelley."

Don took his mob and Ernie Mitchell kept his mob on Yandeyarra and that went on until Ernie Mitchell died. That was before Peter Coppin who took it on after that. Peter Coppin was working with me at that time. He was prospecting for tin at Moolyella. When Ernie Mitchell died, Peter Coppin became the manager out there. Pippingarra's the same, that belongs to them too.

Then McLeod, after they started, bought the Strelley Station off Peter Miller, his father, old Les. There were twenty four thousand sheep on Strelley. The number didn't last too long. It all went in the fire, all went in the pot. Then they bought Carlindie. Well, I think it was through the grants from the government. Then they got Lalla Rookh Station, through the government grants too, of course. That had sheep.

Then they got Warralong Station. They cleaned up the sheep in the saucepan and got cattle there. Then they got Bungalow. They call that Coongan now.

They had no time for sheep, too costly. To run a sheep station, you've got to look after water, have plenty of water, plenty of fences, windmills and tanks. That all costs money. With cattle you only have one well here and one over there — about ten miles away. You don't need fences for them. They just walk anywhere at all.

Don McLeod's mob got Callawah too. They bought that off old Ray Darlington and that was all the stations they got through the government grants. They're still out there, though I don't know how they're getting on or anything like that, I couldn't say. But they got cattle, although I don't know about Callawah. That's an awful country for cattle. It'd be alright for sheep.

In 1948, I worked at a place they call Billjim, twenty-four miles east of Nullagine and Blue Spec. It was full of antimony. Now the antimony is no good with gold. It kills the silver through the battery. You lose a lot of gold. So that was no good. You only found gold where there was no antimony, it's black. That's the only place I know where there's any quantity. They've got some use for it now, but they didn't those days. They were after the gold. They had to send the concentrate to Port Kembla in New South Wales to get it treated again, to get the gold out of it.

I worked there on the Ball Mill, still mining. That was a terrible job that. All the balls were made out of cast iron. You had to weigh every single one, one by one, and whatever weights they were, you had to put them down and what time of the day and so on. Sometimes you had to change them about four times, put a new lot in four times a day, because they wear out. I got one of my thumbs cut there, I had to go to hospital. I got that fixed and went back again. I worked there for about ten months.

When that company ran short of money, I went back and worked with the Stirling Goldmine, that's out from Marble Bar. We were there for quite a while. We wasn't working mines or anything like that, we were just doing odd jobs here and there. It wasn't much good either, but it was something. I got a few bob, not much. After that, I done whatever work I came across. There was no picking your job, you took what you could get.

14

After the strike (1950-63)

Backwards and forwards

In 1950, I went and worked for Mark Rubin Company on Mulyie Pastoral Station, me and my family. They owned five stations. De Grey, Shaw River, Mulyie, Ettrick and Warrawagine. Warrawagine was owned by Mark Rubin. It was Mark Rubin Estate. These other places down here — De Grey, Mulyie, Ettrick and Shaw River, they're a De Grey River Pastoral Company, but they was still Mark Rubin's, owned by him.

He had thirteen stations altogether, including the ones in Queensland. Thirteen — cheap labour, you know. You see, once the Aboriginal people went on strike, the stations just went down like that. They couldn't get cheap labour anymore so they gave us a job. They couldn't pay much, but they made sure they was paying us a bit, basic wage. That was twenty-eight quid a month. Them other fellas, the other blackfellas that was there before us, half-caste fellas too, they were getting nothing or only a little bit. Two quid a month, bread and jam or a bit of shirt and trousers once a year or something like that, practically nothing.

These squatters up here, they're terrible people in the early days. They work you for nothing and give you poor tucker, food was very poor, hardly any wages, no wages in a lot of cases. That's how they build up the stations. No expenses, it kept on going like that until 1946, when the blackfellas all woke up and went on strike. Then when they got us, they had to do something, they gave us a job and paid us basic wage.

I worked with them on and off for thirteen years, all sorts of work, mustering for sheep, fencing, putting up new fences, putting up new yards, fixing old yards and doing a bit of blacksmithing. There was no arc welding or any of that sorta thing. Those days, it all had to be done by forge, hammers and that, blacksmithing, done a lot of that work.

From there, I went down south again. I worked for Bell brothers clearing at Kwinana for the oil refinery. When we finished there, we went to Red Hill and worked there for the same mob until I pulled out. They had plenty of money, they wasn't short of money. But they didn't pay. They were a funny mob. They own some of these trucks here, Bellways. Their sons own them.

After that, we came back to Mulyie. Most of the kids had finished schooling by then. We only had two left to go to school, that was Ronnie and Doreen. All the others was just finished, four of them was finished before we come there. There was a governess on Mulyie who used to teach the boss's children and ours too. We had plenty of work, all stock work and fencing. We didn't have to pay for food because we were getting it free, but when Eggenman came we had to pay for our food. We were also getting the home for free plus twenty-eight quid a month. We were quite alright there, happy.

In 1957, I went into business with a fella down there at a place called Bellevue, out from Midland Junction. Yeah well, he said, "What about a permanent partnership with me?"

I said, "Oh, what doing?"

"Getting old cars, wrecking them and selling spare parts to different ones."

I said, "Alright."

So I did that.

We started a wrecking garage, getting all the old motor cars, get them for nothing just about. I was there for about ten months but I got no money for it, no money. He took all the money! He'd just give me a little bit now and again to keep me alive, to get a bit of food and that. I had to keep my family. Of course by that time, the family had grown up, you know. I only had Ronnie and Doreen to look after. So I got sick of that. I couldn't get no money much, so I walked away, I caught the plane and came back.

I went over to Wallareenya Station. Then I went back to Mark Rubin, Mulyie again for about eight months. He was a poor man then. He didn't have much money. I did some more work there. Then down to De Grey and back to Mulyie and Ettrick. I was backwards and forwards all the time. At Warrawagine, I done a bit up there, done a bit of cooking up there. Well, I was off-siding for my wife while she was doing the cooking. All the children was grown up then and started to look for themselves, you know, keep themselves. So it was only me and the wife left.

We left Warrawagine, went back to De Grey, done a bit of work there. Then they wanted me back at Warrawagine. I went back there for a little while, might've been for four months, four months work.

I went back to Limestone Station out from Marble Bar and they called me back to Mulyie, done a bit more work there. I was there not too long that time, about three, four months and then I had to go back to De Grey and done about the same there, about four months. Backwards and forwards all the time.

I was a sort of spare part doing jobs, odd jobs, and some big heavy jobs too. But they paid alright, they paid a proper wage, barring fencing, that was contract.

Well, one station owner, he paid me thirty quid a mile and the bloke on the next station who belong to the same firm, he was getting sixty pound a mile. I was only getting thirty quid a mile. Well, he just about finished himself now. All those fences that I seen, I been out there not long ago, they're all finished, broken, windmills broken up. They took all the money out of it and bought places down in Perth or something like that. They put nothing back on the place to keep the place going, oh no. That's the trouble going on up here now.

Anyhow, I got sick of that and they started to cut down employment. So I left Mark Rubin Pastoral Company altogether and went looking for another job. That was in 1963.

I went back to Limestone Station, did a bit of work there for about twelve months. They couldn't pay. They paid what they could pay. What bit of money they had was spent on wages and food until they couldn't carry on.

Then I worked bits and pieces. You know how you go, they'll employ you for a little while, then you have to look for another job and so on.

Done a bit of prospecting in the meantime, all over the place. I was after gold, tin and beryl. Beryl is a mineral. It has six corners, you might get a big piece, you might get a long piece. But it has six corners. It's no square, it's a hexagon. I prospected for everything, whatever I could make a living out of.

15

Recognition at last

One sack in my life

Then Kathleen Investment bought Moolyella Tin Mine, what they called the Pilbara Tin Field. There is a place called Tageban. One day, the manager asked me could I take him there to show him the waterhole. A big waterhole comes over the cliff there, always full of water with fish in it.

I said, "Okay."

I had a Landrover, but he said, "No, we'll go on the company's one, save yours."

I said, "Okay." It was eight miles over there.

So when we get out there, went out quite good, but when he switched her off at the pool, at Tageban, we couldn't start her up again. She wouldn't. Battery went flat, got a shortage from somewhere.

It's eight or nine miles to the Pilbara Tin Treatment Plant from Tageban. So from then I just worked around the mine. My job was looking for the best tin about. It was a good job.

There was a team of men working two shifts. I'd just drive around, supervising you know, didn't do much work myself, only work my head.

Caratti, he was an Italian contractor. He had the earth-moving equipment, Mick Caratti was his name. He had a lot of machinery out on the field where we was working. His manager up here was a German fella. I used to work with him, Peter Woll. Well, Peter Woll used to tell me, "Well you know Jack," he said, "my mother and father's in Germany."

I said, "Oh yes."

"He is a bricklayer."

"Oh yeah."

"He's got a hotel over there, so I'm going over in about a month time for a holiday, but I'll be back. I hope you're here."

I said, "Oh, I'll be here. As long as the mine is here, Kathleen Investment, I'll be still here. I'm a bloke that don't shift from one job to another so quickly. I've only had one sack in my life."

When he came back, he started off again. There were two scrapers, three bulldozers, a couple of front end loaders and a mob of trucks. I was in charge of them all. I'd tell them where to go, what to do, how deep to go down and all that sorta thing. They'd cart the dirt into the big mill at Moolyella.

That's supposed to be where I was born. The real Aboriginal name for that is Mulala. Mulala — your nose.

There's these two hills, oh there's lots more, but them two hills, they shed all the tin everywhere. There is one creek, the Moolyella Lead, then Karen's Lead and Huntsmen Gully. On the other side, there's Grady's Gully and McDonald Lead comes around. It goes south and turns right around and comes back north again. The two main hills are two granites. Mulala. You see, Mulala also means the end of everything. Mulamula, that's the end of it. The end is Mula. The finish. You can't go anymore. That's Mulala, that's where I was born.

I stayed with Kathleen Investment and Surveys for five years. Good pay, course I didn't live there, my home was in Marble Bar, sixteen miles in. I used to travel out sixteen miles in the morning, they paid for all that, all the expenses, like the petrol, I didn't pay for that. Only the Landrover was mine, 1975 model it was.

In 1969, the place started to break up, you know, it got sold to somebody else and then Alan Bond bought it. He had quite a few out there working. He worked there for about two years and pulled out. The mine is idle since then.

I went fossicking for tin again. I did alright. I used to get fruit tin full of tin a day, sometimes two. Well, a fruit tin was worth twenty dollars. If I got on a good patch, I might get two, two fruit tins full, that's clean tin.

Well, that's alright. You're your own boss, you can work when you like and how you like, you know. From there I went on exploration jobs for a little while, not long. For Catman Surveys in Hedland, all around the Pilbara, looking at the country, pegging leases and one thing and another like that. If the ground was very rich, well, I'd peg it for the company. I had a Landrover, their Landrover, not mine. At that time, they'd start to do a bit of cheating, you know what cheating means, didn't like to pay out any money. I wasn't being paid properly, so I gave up the job.

My wife died then, in 1977. She died in January, the 5th of January at half past four in 1977. I've been single ever since and will probably be that way all the time.

I went and did a bit of prospecting again, prospecting for gold around Marble Bar and Nullagine area. I went around North Pole Goldmine. I didn't do any good, it was more or less just a bush holiday, you know. Plenty of wild camels, donkeys, they're all over the place. Got a bit of gold, but wasn't worth much, you know, not enough.

I got a mate with me, a white chap, he was single then. I showed him a couple of places and he turned around and sold them to a company. He done all right too, when he got a few bob. Before that, he went drilling over at the Philippines. When they finished drilling there, they went to Egypt. They were drilling there for a long time. Then he came back. While he was overseas, he fell in love with a Filipino girl there. He's got her now, he went back and he got her in Perth now.

He went back after, he thought he'd try his luck and these other mob was silly enough to buy it off him. They got nothing. I got a thousand dollars from one place, but there was another place and I got nothing there.

Yes, oh he had gold leases everywhere. A very nice bloke though, just the same, very nice friend. He was around Marble Bar, around on Warragine, De Grey, Mulyie, all around. He was a dinky-di Australian, you know. He really come from Belmont. That's where his mother and father was.

So we went up to the Kimberley once. We went up the Kimberley for the South Mount Surveys, up past Derby, Fitzroy Crossing. Went out looking for uranium and other things, you know, whatever we could find. There was one place there, but it was pegged by someone else, by a fella called Shanleys.

We went to a pace they called Margaret River. It was very rough out this country, no good for motor car, you got to walk and some places you can't even walk. All the stones was sticking straight up, very sharp, you know, very tough. We found a bit of mineral but it was no good though, only just jasper, that's all. That's on the Margaret River, the place name is Gogo, out from Fitzroy Crossing.

We didn't do any good, I knocked off. I didn't go anywhere for anybody. I came down to Port Hedland, that was in 1982. By that time my eldest boy, John, died in Alice Springs. He was driving buses over there in Alice Springs.

I didn't get my pension until I was seventy-seven. I didn't worry about it before. The pension wasn't too high. Somewhere around about twenty-five, thirty dollars a week or something like that. I lived with my daughter for a little while, Marie, she's the oldest. She lives in Roebourne now. Ithamagaduna, Aboriginal name.

Then I left, went over to her son's place. They had a three bedroom place in South Hedland over in Pedlar Street, not far from Pundulmurra College. They had no children, only him and his missus. I stayed with them for about one year and I put in for a house. Had a job to get one! I got a place down at Edkins Place. I had grandchildren with me, Danny, David and Raymond until they went their own way. So that left me there on my own in the three-roomed house, you know family house. I was still paying rent, so Homeswest couldn't hunt me out or anything. I had put in for a pensioner unit and I got one. I lived there until 1990 and moved into my own house then.

I been to Perth and all that sorta thing. I wrote that book with Sally Morgan, we started on that in 1982 I think it was, but it took many years to do it. We were too far away from each other, you understand, so we got through it in the finish. It took us four years to do it. We launched that book on the 27th September, 1989. I was very happy with it.

16

Old class, old people

I am the last

Well there are lots more stories but we'll be here forever. I am 87 years old now and anything can happen, you know what I mean. This has been going on for three years and I really want to finish it now. The people I talk about are all gone, all gone now.

I am the last.

So let's finish this book properly — from the sea to the desert. All that was the Oakover, you know, whitefellas people called it De Grey, but it wasn't, it was the Oakover. Braeside was at the edge of the desert. It had open country to the north and open country to the south, you know, no stations.

That's where my mother and aunties — there were five sisters — worked for Mrs Hodgson. Nobody really knows what happened to Hodgson. All they know is he jumped out the back window. There are many stories of what happened to him, but no one really knows.

I worked hard all my life until I got my pension. I worked on gold, on batteries. I worked on sand jerking, all sorts of jobs, blacksmithing, a little bit of mechanical work and a lot of truck driving. We had to use horses meant for the job, you know. No such things as motor cars, motor bikes, aeroplanes and helicopters.

I had six children and they all went to school in Marble Bar. There was no school when we were kids. In the early days, if we didn't work we'd get jailed. Not only me, but other young fellas too. We had to work for our living. Even if it was just for tucker, never mind about money, that was forgotten. We were lucky to get money. We might get a shirt and trousers once every six months, sometimes only every twelve months.

Not like now where there's no need to work. There's none of this sitting down waiting for money to come in from the government. Oh there's none of that! Today you can just sit down and get your money. That's why there's a lot of these young fellas when they leave school, just go home, save up and get a flash motor car or something like that for nothing. There was none of that those days.

The motor cars were flash, but not as flash as these today. Old T-model Fords, old Dodges, Chevs, Graham Paiges, Internationals, you don't see those buses now. They all died out. There was no Japanese buses in those days. They're all Americans and English or German buses and you had to work hard to get one!

Most of these youngsters now don't learn about the culture and are getting in jail and one thing and another. They're doing wrong things. It's very very hard to keep them way off it.

The younger generation, you understand, like these young people, they can't speak their own language, they don't understand it, you understand. All they know is drink, waste money, and they'll never work while they get dole money, most of them anyway. And the girls are all mucked up and they're just as bad as the boys. They're not like the old class, old people. They don't take any notice of any people that knows anything, that's had any experience, likes of me or someone over forty-five or something like that. Somebody like them — that, they'll listen to them, but these they won't. They won't work, they won't listen to anything. As long as they can get that free money, that's it, that's what they want.

Even the white class is very near the same now, very near the same. They do do a little bit better than the Aboriginal ones. The Aboriginals, if they had a very very easy job like I know around about here, they'll stick to that, mostly the girls. They seem to stick to it. But the boys, well, there's not too many of them that does stick to it. I've watched them, studied them. They can't walk across the road over there, they are that full!

But there's a reason for that too, I won't say what it is, I won't tell you, let people find out for themselves. It can't last forever and ever, don't matter how good it is.

It's a lot of strain on the government to try and keep them into order. They are helping them, like putting up lovely homes and all that sorta thing, but the Aboriginal people don't see that. I mean the young people, not the old people. The young people, they don't see that sort of thing. They not seem to be interested in it, walk in the house, no principle. Walk in the house and never even tap on the door, "Can I come in?" or anything like that. No, just walk straight in.

So I feel sorry for them but it's not worthwhile. You can't do anything about it I don't think. They won't listen. Bodies getting in the motor car. Look at those fellas now from Jigalong to here. They mob, there must have been fifty of them on one Toyota here one day in front of Coles. You've only got to have one blow-out, a blow-out, they're gone! They don't think of those sorta things, they don't think of danger.

Just one thing, that's alcohol and making nuisances of themselves.

If you only open your eyes and see what's going on around down near Coles — oh you see them outside too — that's all they want. You never see them pushing a pram out, not too many of them, pushing a trolley out with a load of shopping. No, no, they might be, if some of them do, they have a carton down below and cover it up with other. No, that's what I know. I'm speaking the truth about that. There's no way that I can see how they're going to live. They've lost their languages, they can't speak. Of course some of them that doesn't drink, lost their languages too.

Now the cemetery over there, they've already put an extension on it. In another three or four years, they'll have to put another extension on it, make it wider. It'll be over at the airport soon. Most of them is Aboriginal people, not very many whites. There are some whites there but they are old people, old age, but not through alcohol. Aboriginals through alcohol.

See, before they got their free rights, it wasn't so bad, but since they got that in Yandeyarra or anywhere else, they got their own cemeteries. If they had buried them all here, they wouldn't have had any room. They'd be outside.

No, I don't agree with that type of law at all. They got some good boys gone west through alcohol, that's the worse thing that ever was invented amongst them anyway.

Whites, well they are not too bad. They used to be bad one time, but they used to drink hard stuff, spirits, things like that, you know what I mean. But today what I see of them, they are very very good. They have a can when you knock off in hot weather like this, or two cans and finished. Then you have your clean up, shower and have your meals, you don't have anymore. But if you have another one, one for the road sorta business, no that's no good.

I don't like it. That's all, don't like the situation. That's why I live here by myself, I won't allow them to come here. I won't have them. I'm not running them down, I'm only saying the truth about them with alcohol. If they could only leave that, they'd be good men, they'd be good. Go and do their work. There's plenty of work about.

In my time, we got very little money. We might've only got five bob a week, ten bob a week, some got nothing. Only shirt and trousers every six months, pair of boots, something like that too. But we had to work for our food, to live, but nowadays they go cadging for meals. They waste their money on alcohol, alcohol is the main problem.

I've worked with all types of people, I'm talking about especially white people, Scots, Irish, Germans, all sorts of people, but they're totally different. They go in — say, we might be working twenty mile away from the pub — go in once a fortnight, have a good bust-up and that's finished. You don't have anymore until you go in again for a holiday, but then you're away from your job.

But while you're working, work and leave the alcohol alone and do your work! Now, there's work about, it mightn't be much good but it's a job, you understand what I mean. It's a job. Now, all these stations around here, most of them, well all of them you might as well say, put it that way. They were all painted with one brush, they're all built up by Aboriginals — get little or nothing for it. The managers or the owners, they'll have a jackaroo. He wouldn't do anything, but he'd be the boss, see.

All these stations, everywhere along here, been built up by them, the poor bloomin' Aboriginal. He had to do it and there are people now wonder why did they go on strike. They wonder why they did that for. They blamed Don McLeod, he was only just the "talk to", the "ask him now and again". Or if they got papers or anything like that, he'd read it out to them, those that can't read. That was all.

That's why they went on strike. For better conditions. Now they've got it but those that did go on strike, is nearly all dead. Now there's younger generations, well they're no good, no good at all. They don't go both ways. I go the white way and I go the Aboriginal way too. What I mean is this. I listen to what the whitefellas say. I listen to what the blackfellas say. I try to understand and respect both ways. I don't believe in what they do. I do believe, I think they should give up alcohol and go and do a bit of work. Do something for themselves. If they don't want to work for someone, well try — which they can get it now from the government — the grant, loan, whatever it is and they can try and do something for themselves.

Now see, they're trying to run a station on a modern scale. They hire a helicopter or aeroplane, light planes, you know, to gather up the cattle when they're mustering, when they're gathering them up. It's pretty expensive, whereas in my time, we had none of those sort of things.

But I do believe the helicopter is the right thing to get them out in the hills where the horses can't gallop. A lot of cattle are gone wild. They get in these gorges and you can't get around them with horses but with a helicopter you can. You can go right nearly on top of their backs and follow them out. I reckon a helicopter is just the thing.

Some of them, they're coming good. They're coming good slowly, like both sides. The Aboriginal side with the Aboriginal culture and the whites...some of them, they're very, very good.

They're doing alright!

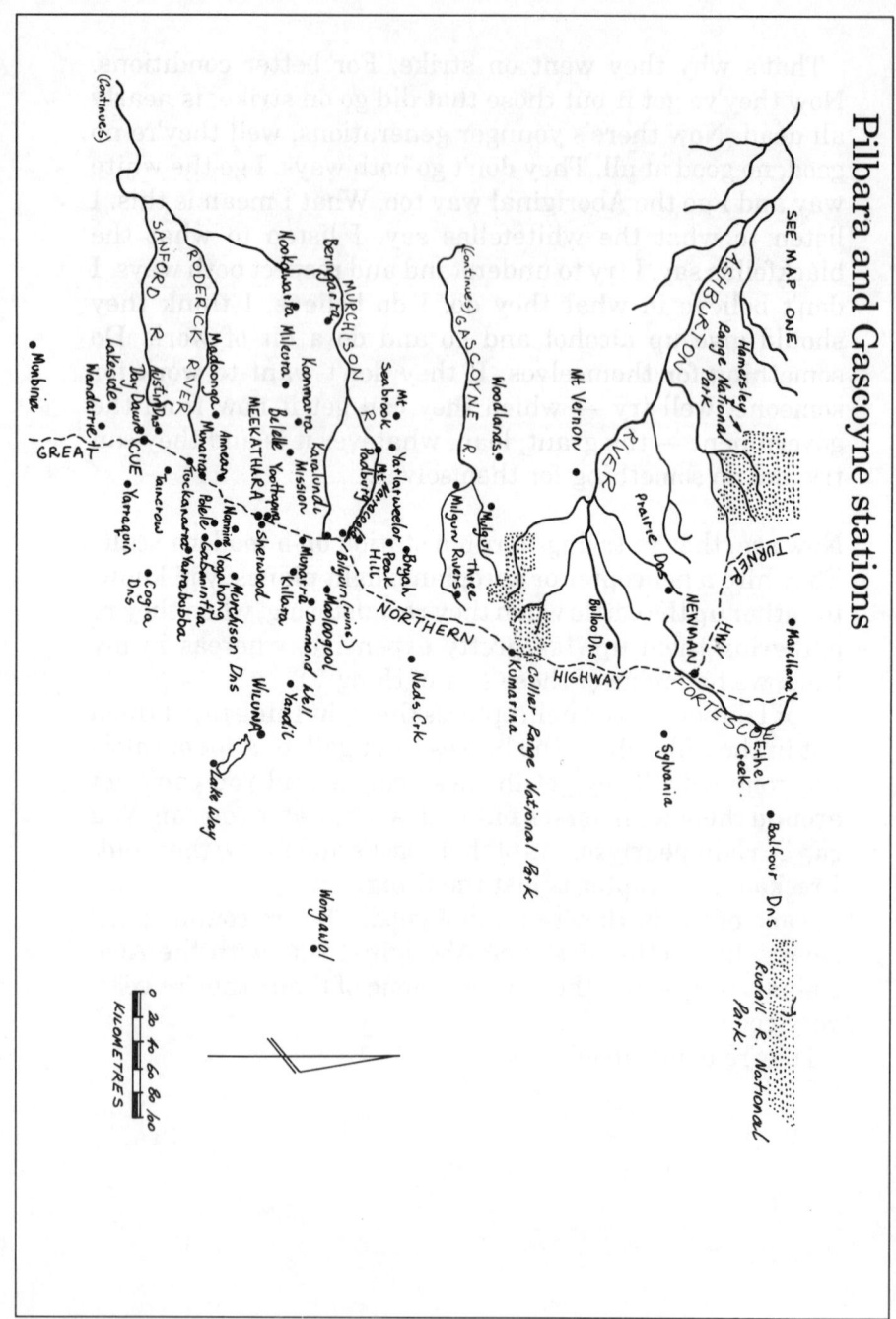

Pilbara and Gascoyne stations

Glossary

All place names in Nyamal language, unless otherwise specified.

Aboriginal	English place names	Literal Translation
Biltinha	Green Waterhole	
Binbiyanha	Binbiana (Jack 1934)	Kangaroos
Braydayirdi	Braeside	A pool at Braeside
buliyuriya		black carpetsnake
Burunguna	Two Trigs Homestead — Meentheena	Tribal name of place, may mean 'nothing over there'
Dabadaba	Tabba Tabba Creek	Derived from English
Daradara	Tarra Tarra Pool,	Split
(see earlier place names)	Roebourne	
djulugu		shoot, hit
Kalambaranha	God's Creek or Gorge Ck.	A place where there is always water
Kaldubudamunha	9 Mile, a creek coming into Coongan River	Plant, with runners, cucumber-like fruit, early settlers pickled these
Kalgawarrana	Shaw Gorge	A break in the gorge
Kaliyri	Carlindie Station	A creek with no trees
Kaludunha	Lalla Rookh Goldmine	Big mountain
Kandimada	Warralong	A Warralong tree Bee Hill
Kandulangu Naruwara	Davis River	Davis River passes it
Kapinuga	Pool near Meentheena	Home of fish
Karawayinha	Carrawine Gorge	Big cliff, large pool below
Karimarra		skin group classification
Karlamilyi	Telfer	Remote desert location
kudu		short
Kudunggayinha	Cuttangunnah Pool	Take me up there
(Ngarla language group)		
Kukunha	Muccan Station	Devils
Kulgangunha	Hillside	Black Range
Kuliyalakabunha	Junction, Tabba	Someone speared there
(Ngarla language group)	Tabba Ck, Marble Bar Rd.	
Kuliyaranha	South Hedland	Cadjebut tree bark. "The whole way"
Kulkunba	Noreena Downs	Where two rivers split.
Kumpayinha	Shag Pool	Birds with long beaks & legs. White and bl. (app. herons)
Kungkanba Naruwara	Coongan River	Meaning lost
kurlkura		head hair
Kurlukurlu Kayinha	Cooracooraniwe Pool, near Chukuwaylee	Laughing jackass
Kurrunha	The name of the pool,	Deep waterhole with
(Ngarla language group)	De Grey Station	branch projecting
Kurutjumaya	Pool on Gregory Creek	House full of ticks
Kutjinamunha	Googhenama	Big waterfall at desert margin
Madagura	Lalla Rookh	One little pinnacle, hill
madugu		spiritual, truly; cf tua

Magadungani	Fig Tree Waterhole	Figtrees grow there
Magari	Elsie Creek	Dead, grave
Malyilirin	Mulyie Pool	Cool
Malyimalyi	Mulyie Station	Nice and cool
mandu		meat
Mandulgari	42 Mile Creek	Creek, w. plenty of meat on it
Maralga	Cooke Bluff Hill	Devil Devil
Maramalangunha	Mt Cometei Pinnacle Pyramid Hill	A hand
marandu		a large type of goanna
MarapiKurinha	Port Hedland	Five Fingers. Refers the five creeksincl. harbour
Marlgunthanha	Mt Edgar	A big black hill comes up
Mamalongunha	Mt Cometei Pinnacle	
Mikapalina	Pear Creek	Emu
Milbingatji	Rockhole next to Walganya Lead Mine	Blood
Milgana	Merrycan Rockhole	Long cave, rockhole, granite country. A lot of water snakes live there
Minangarangu	Miningarra Creek	Related to an arm
Mitjinggatji	Midgengadge Pool	Meaning unknown
Mitjitjimaya	Lockenbah Station	The missus' house
Mugari	Elsie Creek	Meaning unknown
mulamula		end of it
Mulhala	Moolyella	Along the nose. End of everything
Muluna	Muluna Rockhole	Meaning unknown
Mungkumungkunba	White Quartz Hill	Big pool with white ants next to Yarrie Station
Munukudayinha	Warrie Station	At the end of the river
Murlganya	Lock Hospital	First born, oldest child
Ngalangkanu Naruwara	Nullagine River	They're going back on river
Ngukunungha	Mt Divide	Chest here
Ngulimunha	Corunna Downs	Itchy nose, blinking
Nilguna	Yilgalong Pool	Meaning unknown
Paburuna Naruwara	Oakover River	Plenty of water
Palgaramaya	Wallareenya	A house on level ground
Pananggara Manda	Black Rock in Sea	Hillreef rock
Pangkabarra Naruwara	Shaw River	Stalks of spinifex
Pawura	Bonney Downs	Buck spinifex
Pilawa	Mayola	A war was held there
Pilimara	Petermarer Creek	Chest-hand
(Kariyarra language group)		
Pilimaya	Callawah Station	Old people's houses
Piliyin Piliyin	Billin Ballin Rebble	Meaning unknown
Pindunha	Pinda Post Office	Little cliff there
Pinpinba	Pin Pin Creek	Bowerbird nest
Pipayana	Davis Ave, Marble Bar	Old girl is buried there
Pipingara	Beebingarra Creek	Meaning unknown

Puda-Pudara	Mt Hodgson	Black bungarra
Pudapudara	Twelve Mile	Black bungarra
Pulpulgarra	Kobbler Pool	Cat fish, kobblers
Pulyiri	King Rockhole	Budgerigar
Pulyirrina	Twenty Ounce	Shell parrot
Pununggadayinha	Shady Well, a pool	Name of the pool near Surprise Goldmine
Purungu		skin group classification
Tadibanha	Tageban Pool	A big rockhole is there
Tadunuga	Limestone Ridge near Noreena Dns, Milbina Pool	Home of the marchfly
talangayanguna		where are you gone?
Talgunha	Finucane Island	Cadjebut tree
Talgu Talgu Naruwara	Talga River	Cadjebut trees
Taliyaranha	Mt Woodhouse	Spring surrounded by many weeds
Tandinha	Ettrick Station	An island comes in
Tangalina	Coppin's Patch Goldmine	Gold
Tambutambunha	Long Pool	Dead Logs
Tarapuna	Triangle Pool	A permanent pool
Thingaraganya	Lambing Creek or Young Hodgson's Creek	Tall thin straight trees
Thuliya	Marble Bar	End of the ranges
Tjidamuna	Duffer Creek	Meaning unknown
Tjidanamunha also"Pawura"	Tabletop Hill with breakaway near Bonney Downs Station	Place name, at sundown 'moving hole' seen in hill related to Mangalirgurla, animals living there. One can never get close or they'll disappear
Tjidangamunha	Bamboo Springs	Two creeks joining
Tjilumbunha	Balfour Downs	Fruit looking like small apples, on little bushes
Tjiritjiridanha	Eel Pool	Black Willy Wagtail
Tjukawalyi	Chukuwalyee Pool	Bad Sugar
tua		mother-in-law rel'nship; facing or approaching forbidden
Tulunha	Doolena Gorge	Name of old blackfella
Tuma	Tooma	Meaning unknown
Tungkunalatji	Running Waters	Two creeks coming in
Tungkunyinha	Pardoo	First part of word means' back', second unknown
Turali	Strelley	Nothing but spinifex there
Wabilgul	Old Port Hedland Cemetery.	Name of the person who's buried there
wakuburu		fighting stick
Walala	Nimingarra Station	Hill near Shay Gap
Waldurara	Telfer	Black range stretches out
Walganya	Lead mine on Dingo Creek.	Lead
Walyurigari	Mt Sydney	No man's land
Wambugambuna	Wongewobbin Pool next to Pindah P.O.	Junction of Nullagine-Oakover Rivers

Wanamarraganya *also* *Wanamurragunya*	A spring on Mt Edgar Creek.	Wanamarra: wheatlike plant, grows in water. Onion at base like tiny coconut; food, dried, crushed for flour, makes damper; ganya: Jack's Aboriginal stepfather's grave is there
Wanangkana	Crofton's Well	Meaning unknown
Wandilurruba	Skull Springs	Kangaroo tail
Wandurarra	Mt Crofton	Meaning unknown
Wantjila Karana	Nullagine Gorge	A gap in mountain range
Warugayinha	Warrawagine	Name of pool
Wayinagurlbanha	Cooke Point Ridge From Harbour to Cooke Point	Meaning unknown
Wilbagariganya	Two Sisters	Two sisters, spinifex country.
Wiridinan	Baramine Station	An army came to fight there
Wirndiwirndinha	Windiwindina Pool	Sparrowhawk
Wurupadiri	Woorabardaree Pool	Pool that never goes dry
Wuthu	Shay Gap	Range of hills
Yalama	Place of new hospital now in Port Hedland	Sick people
yamangarina		go(ne) away
Yari	Yarrie Station	Red ochre
Yindayindanha	Pelican Pool, Round Hole	Pelicans
Yiranggadi	Nullagine	(i) teeth; (ii) blade of tomahawk; (iii) sharpen that blade
Yirlirrinha	Goldsworthy	Red ochre
Yugurumindha	Strelley Siding	Dog's nose
yulugadai		to his camp
yuluwali		going home to his camp
YuruKulduna	4 Mile Soak Waterhole near Leslie Salt	Spinifex pigeons

Metric Equivalents

Australian currency was based on the pound or the 'quid', which was converted to $2.00 in 1966. The pound consisted of 20 shillings (20/-) of 12 pence (12d) each. The shilling, or 'bob', was divided into sixpences (6d) or threepences (3d). The shilling was converted to ten cents and sixpence to five cents.

Imperial	Metric	Imperial	Metric
mile	1.61 kilometres	pound (weight)	454 grams
inch	2.54 centimetres	ounce	28.3 grams
feet	30.5 centimetres	gallon	4.55 Litres

Further Reading

Books

Battye, Jas. S. *The History of the North West of Australia – Embracing Kimberley, Gascoyne and Murchison Districts,* V.K. Jones & Co., Perth, Australia, 1915

Boyd, D. *Meekatharra – A Glimpse of the Past: A Bicentennial, Back to Meekatharra Publication,* Meekatharra Shire, Australia, 1988

Gregory, Robert *Early Mining in the Pilbara: Hamersley Iron 1986, the 20th Year of Hamersley Iron Diary,* Hamersley Iron, Perth, Australia, 1986

Hardie, Jenny *Nor' Westers of the Pilbara Breed – The Story of Brave Ancestors who Pioneered the Outback Pilbara in Western Australia,* Hesperian Press, Western Australia, 1988

Heydon, P.R. *Gold on the Murchison – A Tale of Twin Towns: Cue and Daydawn: Of People, Progress and Gold,* Hesperian Press, Western Australia, 1986

Holthouse, Edward *One Life's Journey,* Hesperian Press, Western Australia, 1987

Jacobs, Pat *Mister Neville: A Biography,* Fremantle Arts Centre Press, Western Australia, 1990

Kelly, Shiela M. *The Long Road Back,* Artlook Books, Western Australia, 1988

McLeod, Don W. *How the West was Lost – The Native Question in the Development of Western Australia,* D.W. McLeod, Western Australia, 1984

Morgan, Sally *Wanamurraganya – The Story of Jack McPhee,* Fremantle Arts Press, Australia 1989

Nixon, M. and Lefroy, R.F.B. *Road to the Murchison,* Vanguard Press, 1988

Sligo, N.K. *Mates And Gold – Reminiscenes of Early Westralian Goldfields: 1890-1896,* Hesperian Press, Western Australia, 1980

Uren, Malcolm *Glint of Gold: A Story of the Goldfields of the West,* Angus & Robertson, Australia, 1980

Weller, Helen *North of the 26th,* The Nine Club, West Australian Art Magazine, Artlook Books, Western Australia, 1979

Wilson, Graham. J. *Pilbara Bushman – The Life Experience of W. Dunn,* Hesperian Press, Western Australia, 1980

Materials held by South Hedland Library

Drewery, Roberta J.   Correspondence with J. Hardie, 'Afghan' names, 1978.

Thompson Family   Letter given by Mrs M. Bulyani, written by her Uncle Thompson. Details of events leading to Roslin Matama's conviction, to death

Pamphlets

The History and Development of Port Hedland
Port Hedland Cemetery
Origins of road names within the Shire of Port Hedland
Port Hedland Heritage Trails
Marble Bar

Index

mainly names and places

Key: Battery=Batt.; Certificate=Cert; Creek=*Ck;* Downs=Dns; Goldmine=*Gm.;*
Government=Govt; Homestead=Hstd; Hotel=Htl; Mine=*M.;* River=*R.;*
Rockhole=R'hole; Station=Stn; Treatment=Trmt; Well=*W.;* Windmill=W'ml

Abbots *Gm.* 75
Aboriginal culture;
language; law; way 4-7,22-
  4,36,52,62,74,88,118-24,
  149,151
Adams, Bluey 25-6
Afghans 56-7,73
alcohol 24, 62,72,125,151
Amber, George 61
Anderson, Wlm; Keith 98-9;
  Robt 61
Anna Plains
Annean, Stn 74
Arthur, George 14,17-8
asbestos 134
Ashburton 74
Aspro, Jacky 120-21
Austin Dns, Stn 34,74,76,81

Baker, Billy 107
Bald Hill 31,89
Balfour Dns, Stn 32,73
Ball Mill 138
Balla Balla *see* Roebourne
Bamboo *Ck* 69; Springs, Stn
  72
Bambra 18-9
Bandijim, Mary Anne 3,4
Bandy-Jim 54
Banjo 25
Banjo Pool 30
Barton, Batt., *Gm.* 73,107
Bayes, Tom 73
Bayman, Charlie 61,128
Beagle Bay 33,100
Beart, Alec 66; Arthur 72
Beasley's Big Claypan 29
Beaton 80
Belelle 74
Bell Bros. 140
Benda, Monty 89

Bennett, Peter 131
Beringarra 84
beryl 142
Billet, George 63
Billiluna 132
Billin Ballin 29
Billjim 138
Bilyuin Pool, pub 75
Bin Bin, Dooley 136
Binbiyanha 92,96
Black Range 105
Black Rock 24
Black Tank 28
Blackboy Hill 19
Blair, Chas, Col., Ian, Jean,
  Keith, Thel. 95
Blue Spec 138
Boddington 79
Bond, Alan 145
Bonny Dns, Stn 56,73
Bonnydoon 70
Boodalarie 101
Boodalyerri 107
Boon, Ah 2
Boondah 73
Braeside 29,52,148
Brearley, Capt. 63,98
Bridal Face 31
Bryah 75
Bullara 1,13
Bulletine, The 70
Bullgarina 108
Bulloo Dns, Stn 81,89
Bunandi, Jackie 106
Bungalow, Stn 69,137
Burton, Bill 123
burial, bush 22,49
Byas, Tom 105

Calanjadie Stn 28
Callawah, Stn 56,138

camels 15,24,47,54-6,64,70,
  73,75,93,96,101,108,145
Camel Pool 15
Campbell, & Co 31; Ang. 69;
  Max. 61; Mich. & Co 84
Canning Stock Route 31,75,
  132
Caratti, Mick 144
Carawine, pool 29
Carlindie, Stn 2,15,68,137
Carnot Bay, Stn 33
Carpenter, Dinah 3
Castlemaine 107
Cater, Abdul 57
Catman Surveys 145
Catholics 100
Charlie *Gm.* 70
cheating prospectors *see*
  exploitation
Chessman, George 71
Chinaman 12,26
Chinaman's Pool 72
Christie, Jack 22
Chukuwalyee, pool 28
Church *see* Straker &
Citizenship Rights 100,134
Clarke(s) 99; Jimmy 130;
  Mother 101
Clarkson 72,79
Cogla Dns 80
Collarah 32
Colonial Sugar Refinery131
comet *see* Halley's
Comet *Gm.* 30,129-30,134
conditions, living 101
Condon, *Ck* 24,54,56,70
Conglomerate, Htl. 72; *M.*
  73,126
Conway, Paddy 118
Cooglegong Htl. 52
Coojinarilna *Ck* 36

160

Cookes *Ck* 104,121-22,137
Coongan *see* Bungalow; htl 2,69; R. 13,34,54; Siding 56,108
copper 107,134
Copper Hill 134
Coppin, Ha. 68-9; Herb. 69; Peter 137; Wlm 69
Corbett, Michael, 69
Corboy 72, Des.; Elma 63, 131
Corney, George 68-9
Cornish, Dugal 55
Corunna Dns, air base 130; Stn 63,72
Coyle, George 80
Craig, Jimmy 96
Crameri 60
Crawford, Alan 68
Crofton, Alf 73
cross-branding *see* duffing
Crowden, Ha. 73
Croydon 52
Cue 34,74,76,84
cyclone 102-3

Daily, Bill 70
Dann, Dingo 32; Matt 99-100
Darby, Paddy 106
Darcy, Charlie, Maud 79
Darlington, Ray 138
Davis *R.* 29,95
Day Dawn 76; Htl.
De Bernales, Claude 129
De Grey, *R.* 148; Pastoral Co., Stn 34,47,69,139,141
De Marchi, Ben 69
Depression 77-80,86
Derby 59,63,146
Devonport, Fred 1,108
diamonds 73,107,127
Diamond W. Stn 30
Dick, old 36,45
Dicks, Dr 131
Disappointment 29
Dinah (Aunty) 9,10,52
Dobson of Australia 49-51
Doherty's Reward, *Gm.* 8, 73,117
Doherty, Clancy 9; Jack 9, 96; Mick 8-9,73

Dollypot 69
Dowling, Wally 132
Drake, Jimmy 117
Drake-Brockman 72
droving 88, *passim*
dry-blowing 4,21,85,104, 127,135
duffing, cattle 9,30,89-90
Dunnet, Bill 45
Dwyer, Judge 89-90

Eastern *Ck* 8,73,96,101
eclipse 34
Edies W. 20
Edkins, Place; Rob 68
education *see* school
Eel Pool 29
Eggenman 140
Eginbah 2,56,69
Eighty Mile Beach 25
Eladgie, Springs 72, Stn 31
Elleridge, Barkley 128
Ellery(s), Bill 99
Elliot, Andy 13,71
Elsie *M.* 8
Engine W. 29
England 71
Ethel Ck, Stn 29,55,73,81, 93
Ettrick 56,69,139,141
Eva (Aunty) 4
Evans, George, Johnny 31
Exemption Cert. 100
exploitation 117-27,129,140-42,146

Farber, Ha. 27-31,34-5
Federation *M.* 70
Fig Tree R'hole 96
Fisher, Billy 75
Fitzroy Crossing 146
Foulkes-Taylor 63
Four Mile Ridge 15
Four-By-Two 69
Francis, Doug. 128
Francisco 75
Frazier Dns, Stn 28,88
Fry 84

Gabanintha, Htl. 32,80
Gap, The 74
Garden Gully 75

Gascoyne R. 29
Gerhard (builder) 10-11
German(y) 26,76,104,144
Gibson, Prince 31
Gidgigunna 75
Gilbert, Miss 95
Gillespie, Dr 72
Ginger, old 129
Gogo 146
gold *passim*
Golden Granite 8
Goldfields W.
Gooallan 73
Good, Hadley 73
Goode, Walter 72
Googhenama 96
Gorge *Ck,*htl 2; Hstd 17
governess 95,140
government wells 29-30,72, 104
Grady's Gully 144
Grant 69
Gray, Tommy 130
Great Fingall 76,107
Green, Fred. 108; Harry 70
Greene, Ha. 32
Greenwood, Stn 75,81
Guinness, Davy 73
Gunstock 36,45

Haggett, Sammy 75
Hall, Frank 131
Halley's Comet 10
Hamilton 27
Hancock(s) 73,84
Hanson, Albert 71,129
Hardey 68
Hardies 68; George, Ted, Tom 69
Harp, The 8
Hawks 99
Hayes, Jack 73
Hedditch, Kath., Micky 14; Tom 13-14
Hill Fifty *Gm.*133
Hillside Stn 34,72
Hillview Stn 32
Hodgson 53,148; Mrs 29,53
Hogan, Dr 131
Holdens Find, *Gm.* 75
Holthouse, Charlie 69
Homeward Bound *M.* 70

horses 101,107,132, *passim*
Horses *Ck* 29
Howard, Jimmy 75
Huntsmen Gully 144
Hutchinson, Jack 128

Indee Stn 68
Injaru, Inja 56
Italian(s) 26,70
Ithamagduna 52,147

Jack, Champagne, Rock-
  cake, Sunburnt 65-8
Jackson, Huey 70
Japanese 12,130
Jefferies, Ted 68
Jenkins, Ha. 8
Jiboongunna Pool 29
Jigalong 73
Jimblebar Pool, 29
Jimmy, old 117-20
Jones, Jimmy (Donkey) 30-1
Judmai, Snowy
Jumbo *see* Shakesburg
Just In Time, *Gm.* 126
justice, miscarriage 105-7

kangaroo shooting 77-8
Karalundi 30
Karen's Lead 144
Kathleen Investment 143,
  145
Keanon, Billy 69
Kelly *see* Warden K.
Kennedy, Jack 108
Kerr, Charlie 68
Kimberley 32,132,146
King Tin *Ck* 21
King, Huey 84
Kingsford-Smith, Chas 63,
  98
Kitchener *Gm.* 70
Koepanger 25
Koombana 1,13
Kudu Kudu 60
Kukal *Ck see* Cooke's
Kulalam 56
Kulaluna 93
Kullawarri Windmill 29
Kumarina 72
Kurutjamaya 93
Kurlukurluwayinha 29

La Grange Bay, dip 27
Lake Way (L. Naberoo) 30
Lakeside Stn 79
Lalla Rookh Gm. 19; Stn 68,
  137
Lambing (Young Hodgson's)
  Ck 29
Landrovers 132
Laurie and Jack
law *see* Aboriginal Law
lead 108
Leake, Brumby 88-92; Mary
  90
Lee, Glory, Tommy, Wally
  75
Lennard, Billy 22
Liddelow, Punch 73
Limestone Stn 14,63,141-42
Lindsay 92
liquor consumption *see*
  alcohol
Little R. 29
Little Wonder 129
Lock Hospital 15
Lockyer, Arnold, Arthur,
  Eric, Manny 130
Lombadina 33
Lower Mosquito 105
Luke, Billy 72
Luva, Paddy 121-24
Lynas, Billy 124-27
Lyndon 96

MacIntosh 84
Madoonga 84
Magazine Pool 72
Maher, Black Billy 10-14,
  71
Mahomet 15
Malays 12,25
Malkan, Jim 56-7
Mallett, Tommy 63,70
Mamajong 56
Mannion, Mrs 60
Marapikurrinha 1,100
Marble Bar 2,13,56-9,70-2,
  85,108,126,134-35,138,145
Margaret R. 146
Marillana 73
Marlambool *W.* 28
Marlu Marlu 92
Marter, Sid 56

Martin, Billy 57,87
Martins 7,8
marriage 86,88
Masterson, Tom 8,73
Matama 56
Matthews, Jack 30; Paddy
  32; Sam 95; Tom 13,71
McAllister 70
McDonald Flat 70; Lead 144
McDonald, Billy 70
McGovern, Billy 14,73
McGregor, George 14; &
  Riches 68
McKay 68; Boonga 73; Keith
  62
McKenna, Clancy 136;
  Maurice 9,63,73,131
McKinnon, Alex 2; Billy 126
McLeod's Reward 20
McLeod, Don 136-38,152
McPhee, Alec (Sandy) 1,4,
  18-9,21; Wlm (Billy) 19,21,
  69; Doreen 130,140; Jack,
  Jimmy 19,21; Johnny 93,
  146; Marie 93,147;
  Ronnie 140; Rory 19,21
McPhee's, Batt. 107; Patch
  19
McRae, Billy 75
Meecardagunna, Pool 29
Meehan 77; Alec 32,75;
  Arthur 74; John 80-81;
  Patrick 34; Ned 32,75
Meekatharra 74-8,84; Dam
  77
Meentheena, Stn 9,32,95-6
Micky Two, *Gm.* 70
Midgengadge Pool 29
Migaraganha, pool 29
Mikanna 13

Miles, & Co 73; George 71
Mileura 84
Milgun 30,81
Miller, Les, Peter 137
Mitchell 68; Ernie 137;
  Fred, Jack 93-4
Mogumber Siding 86
Mohammed, Mula Sid 56
Mohammed, Nick 56-9
Moolna R'hole 29
Mooloogool 30

Moolyella 3,137,144; Lead 70,144; tin *M.* 19-20,106, 143
Moore R. Settlement 86-7
Moore, Joe 60-1
Morgan, Sally 147
Morning Star 8,73
Moseley, Athol 61
Mosquito *Ck* 104-5
Mountain Maid *Gm.* 117
Mox *W.*29
Moxon, Billy 108
Mt Edgar, Stn 63,72,108
Mt Frisco 137
Mt Governor 72
Mt Magnet 76
Mt Newman 72; Works 68
Mt Padbury 30,87
Mt Seabrook, Stn 30,84
Mt Vernon 30,74
Mt Yagahong 32,80
Muccan Stn 69
Mulala 144
Mulga Dns, Stn 26,73
Mulgul 30
Mulyie, Stn 34,47,69,139-41
Munarra Govt *W.* 30; Stn 76
Munbinia 81
Mundabullangana 62,68
Mundiwindi 29
Murchison 74; Dns 31
Murphy(s) 99; Tommy 130
Murphy's Gap 21
Murramunda, Stn 73; *W.* 29
Musical Tramp *see* Keanon, Billy
Myers, Walter 70

Naberoo 72 *see* L. Way
Naljee 28
Nambeet *W.* 28
Nannine 74,84
Narracoota 29
Nelson, Tom 73
Nelson's Point 100
Neville, A.O. 86-7,106
New Zealand Pastoral Co. 84
Nichols, Billy 75
Nilguna 4,6
Nimingarra Stn 69
Ninety Mile Beach

Nookawarra 76,84
Noreena Dns 88
North Pole *Gm.* 145
Norwegian 65,71
Nugglegunna 75
Nullagine 56,72-3,101,104-7; Htl. 72; *R.* 105
Nyamal 88
Nyangumarta 88

O'Brien, Con 127
O'Leary, Mick 70
O'Neil, Katie 13,14
Oakover *R.* 5,6,92,95,148
Oberdoo, Jacob 136
Oldfield, Ha. 61
One Mile, Batt. 73
One Tree *W.* 28
outlaws 80-2

Padbury, Mr 69
Paddy's Market 20
Paddy *see* Darby
Palyku 88
Pardoo Stn 69
Parson 71
Paspalas 60
Pattersons 30
Paul, Frank 121-22
pay rates 47,76-7,84,99, 101,131,136,139-42,145
Peak Hill 34,75; Police 90
Pear *Ck* 14
pearling 25
Pearse, Thorton 84
Pedlar(s), Jack, Mort 99
Petermarer *Ck* 2
Piantas 99; Mother 101
Pickard 70
Pidadepina 4-7
Pilbara 132; Tin Field, Trmt Plant 143
Pilga Stn 72
Pilkington, Mrs 60
Pincher 107
Pindah 28
Pippingarra 68
Pirrinha R'hole 96
police 4,11,22,26,45,54,71, 75,80,90,105-6
Poodubullara, Yard 14
Poondina 2,16

Port Hedland 1,2,13,15,54, 70,98,106
Prairie Dns, Stn 30,88-92
processing, gold/silver 101-2,104,134,138
Prophecy *Gm.* 70
Pulpulgara 29

Qua, Aug 2,61
Quansing 2
Quartz, pool 28

Rabbit *W.* 28-9
Rabbit Proof Fence 73
racism 98-100,149, *passim*
Ragged Hills 108
Red Hill 140
Red Water 28
Residential Warden 71, *see* Warden K.
Richardson, Peter 68
Riches *see* McGregor
Road Board 128
Robinson, Conrad, four brothers 69
Roche, Ned 72
Roebourne *see* Ithamagaduna
Rollah Dns Stn 27
Roy Hill, Stn 29,58,73,93
Rubin, Mark 68-9,139,141
Ruby *W.* 30
rum-tasters 24,72
Running Waters 29

Saddlegunna 29,75
Sarin
Savory *Ck* 29
school 13-4,35,71,95,99, 126-28,135,149
Scrymgour, Jack 71
Shag Pool 29
Shakesburg, Robt 75
Shanley (s) 146, Andy 71
Sharks Gully 20-1
Shaw R., Stn 2,139
Sherwood Stn 75
Shiloo, Ernie 73
Shire Council 71
Singhalese 25
Skeen, Jack 83
Skull Springs 29,93-6

Smith, Chas 73,81; Jack &
Laurie 83; Jim & Co 73;
Wlm 73,106
Snell(s) 72; Bill 31
Sorenson 104-6
Souey 2
Sth Mt Surveys 146
Spalding, George
Spinifex W. 29
Split Rock Stn 55
Sprigg, Ha. 74; Hen. 31
Spring Vale 75
Squatters 47,140
Stanley, Jack 68
State, Batt. 70,74,126;
Shipping Service 60
station, family 95; practices,
work, diet 45-9,64-5,83,
137,140; starting a 92-7
Stewart, Jeff 73
Stewart's Garden 13
Stirling *Gm.* 138
Straker & Church 76
Strapp, Corporal 9-10,71
Stray Shot 11
Strelley, Gorge; *R.;* Stn 68,
137
strike, Pilbara 136,140,153
Stubbs, Stuart (Stubbsy)
134
Swan, Archie 108
Swinton, Freddy 74
Sylvania 73,81

Tabba Tabba, Stn 68
Tageban 143
Taincrow 80
Talga (Talga Talga), *M.*
20-1; *R.* 19; Stn 56,70
Tamborah 52
Tanderlini, Micky 70
Taplin, Len 62-3,98-9
Tarra Tarra 95-6
Taylor 72, Lionel 108
Thinggaraganya (Lambing
Ck) 53
Thompson 54-5, Alf, Don,
Frank 69; Jack, Joe, Mrs
Rod, Sandy, Wlm, Wlm
Jnr 54
Three Rivers Stn 29
Tiffany 24

tin 4,19-20,70,87,135,144
Toby 36,45
Tong Fatt, Ho 2
Tooma (Tuma), Pool 5,29
Tow, Ah 61
Trembath, Frank 2
Triado, Dr 9
Tuckanarra 76
Tuma *see* Tooma
Turee *Ck* 30
Turner, Bob 71
Twenty Mile Sandy 73,101,
117
Twenty Ounce, Gully 52,108
Two Sisters hills *see*
Wilbagaringanya

uranium 146

VDC 130
Vickers, Dr 61
Vines, Dr Ed. 53

Walker 72; Jack 24
Wallal, Dns, post office, Stn
28,34,50
Wallareenya Stn 141
Wandarrie 76
Walsh, bros 84; Frank 70
Wanggugabunha, pool 28
war 19,21,26,98,130
Warangol 28
Ward *R.* 75
Warden Kelly 11
Warden Ritchie 71
Warralong Stn 36,69,107,
137
Warrawagine Stn 28,32,45,
54-6,69,93,108,139,141
Warrawoona 52
Warrie Stn 72
Water Supply 16,26,28,48,
65-8,72,75,100, *passim*
Watson, Bert 3-4,70
Webster, Jack 61-2
Wehl, Fred 73
Wells, Fred 70
Welsh, Frank 69
Whim *Ck* 52
White Khan *see* Haggett
Wilbagariganya 6-7
wild cattle 96-7

Williams, Frank 9,71
Willie *Ck* 33
Wilsons 60
Wiluna 30,132
Windy Springs 31,132
wolfram 136-37
Woll, Peter 144
Wongawol 30
Woodie Woodie Manganese
M. 7
Woodlands 30
Woodman, Billy, Mr and
Mrs 70
Woodstock 52
Worner 72
Wyndham 59

Yalgoo 81
Yaloginda 76
Yandeyarra, Stn 52,68,107,
137
Yandicoogina 107
Yandil 31
Yarlarweelor Stn 30
Yarrabubba Stn 32,74,80
Yarraquin Stn 79
Yarrie Stn 28,56
Yinadong 28
Yoothapina Stn 75
Young Hodgson's Ck

Zarene 56-7
Zuki 2

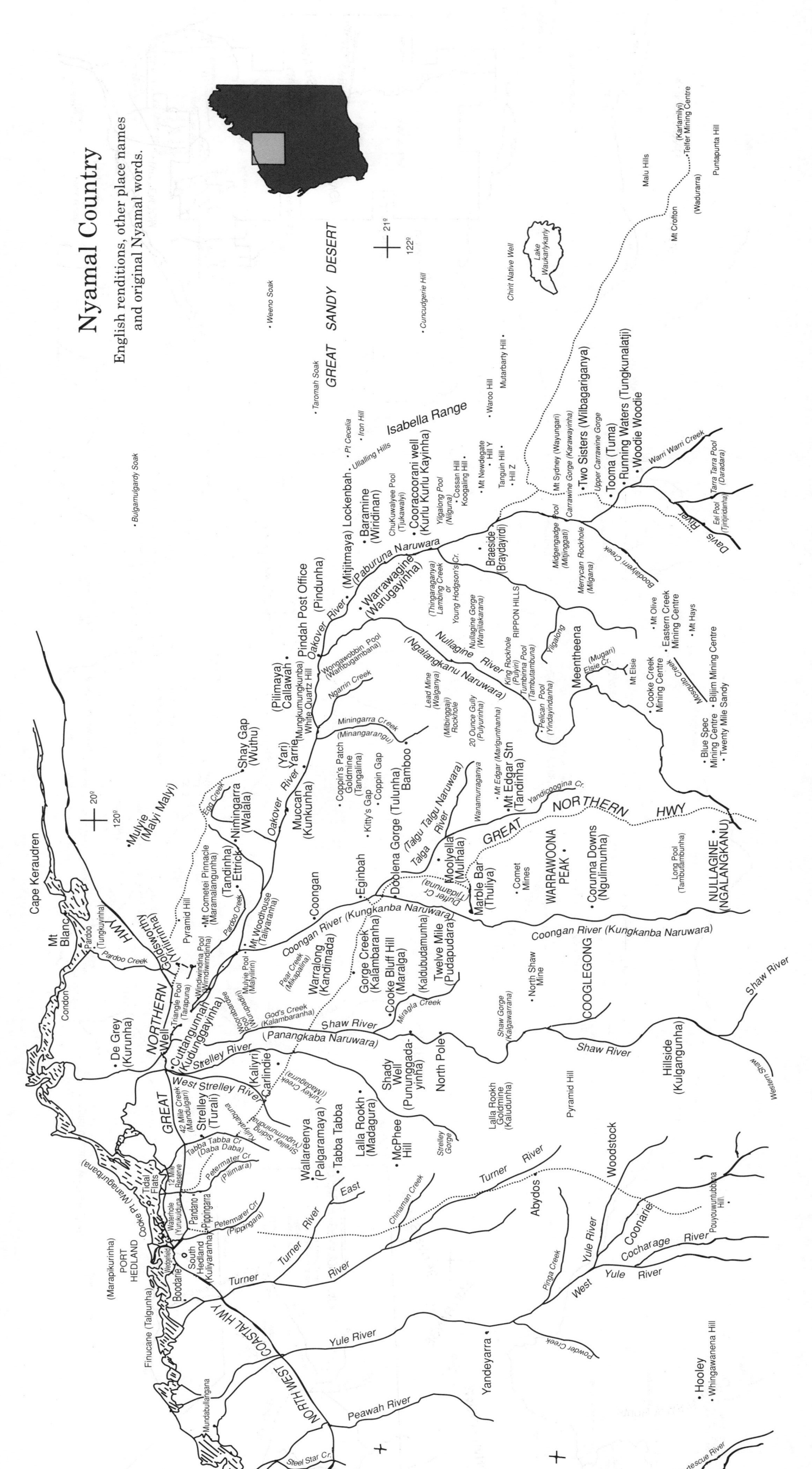

Nyamal Country

English renditions, other place names and original Nyamal words.

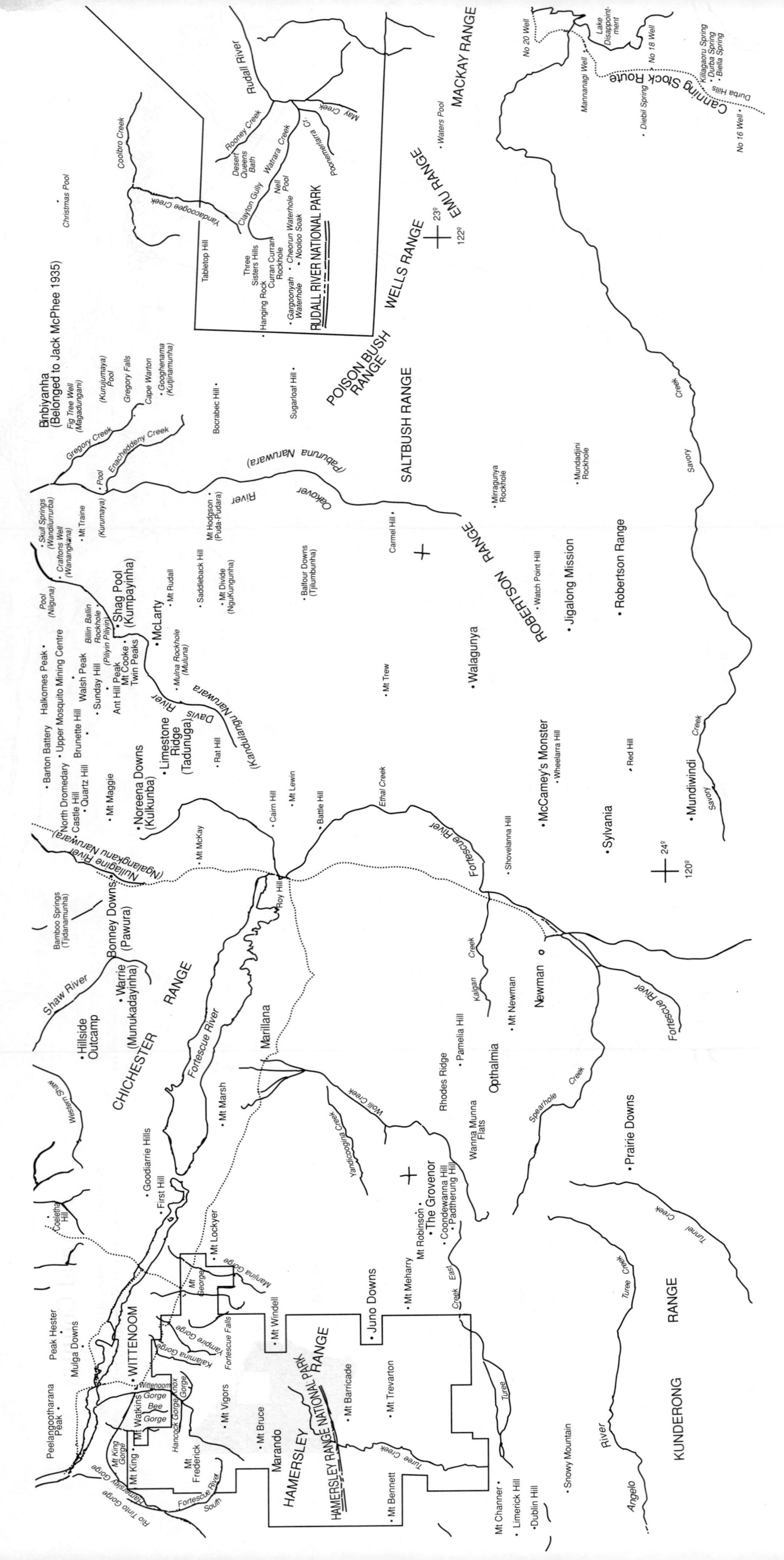

Binbiyanha
(Belonged to Jack McPhee 1935)

Christmas Pool

Coolbro Creek

Yandacoogina Creek

Rudall River

May Creek

Rooney Creek

Desert Queens Bath

Warrara Creek

Clayton Gully

Nell

Curran Curran Rockhole

Cheorun Waterhole

Poonemurrara Ck

MACKAY RANGE

No 20 Well

Lake Disappointment

Killagaoru Spring

Durba Spring

Biella Spring

Canning Stock Route

Mannanagi Well

No 18 Well

Durba Hills

Diebil Spring

No 16 Well

Three Sisters Hills

Hanging Rock

Gargoonyah Waterhole

Nooloo Soak

RUDALL RIVER NATIONAL PARK

Tabletop Hill

EMU RANGE

23°

122°

Waters Pool

WELLS RANGE

Fig Tree Well (Magadungani)

(Kurujumaya) Pool

Gregory Falls

Cape Warton

Googhenama (Kutjinamunha)

POISON BUSH RANGE

Sugarloaf Hill

Bocrabec Hill

SALTBUSH RANGE

Gregory Creek

Enacheddeny Creek

Pabununa Naruwara)

River

Oakover River

ROBERTSON RANGE

Carmel Hill

Watch Point Hill

Jigalong Mission

Robertson Range

Miiragunya Rockhole

Mundadjini Rockhole

Savory Creek

Pool

Skull Springs (Wandilurruba)

Craftons Well (Wanangkana)

Mt Traine

(Kurumaya)

(Kurumaya)

Pool (Nilguna)

Billin Billin Rockhole

Shag Pool (Kumpayinha)

McLarty

Mt Rudall

Saddleback Hill

Mt Hodgson (Puda-Pudara)

Balfour Downs (Tjilumbunha)

Mt Divide (NguKungunha)

Walagunya

Mt Trew

Halkomes Peak

Upper Mosquito Mining Centre

Brunette Hill

Walsh Peak

Sunday Hill

(Pilyin Pilyin)

Ant Hill Peak

Mt Cooke

Twin Peaks

Davis River

Mulna Rockhole (Muluna)

McCamey's Monster

Wheelarra Hill

Sylvania

Red Hill

Barton Battery

North Dromedary

Castle Hill

Quartz Hill

Mt Maggie

Noreena Downs (Kulkunba)

Limestone Ridge (Tadunuga)

Rat Hill

(Kandulannya Naruwara)

Cairn Hill

Mt Lewin

Battle Hill

Ethal Creek

Fortescue River

Shovelanna Hill

Mundiwindi

Savory Creek

Bamboo Springs (Tjidanamunha)

Bonney Downs (Pawura)

Warrie (Munukadayinha)

Nullagine River (Ngalangkanu Naruwara)

Mt McKay

Roy Hill

Fortescue River

Kalgan Creek

Pamelia Hill

Mt Newman

Newman

Spearhole Creek

Prairie Downs

Peelangootharana Peak

Peak Hester

Mulga Downs

Shaw River

Hillside Outcamp

Coeletha Hill

First Hill

Goodiarrie Hills

CHICHESTER RANGE

Western River

Marillana

Wolli Creek

Rhodes Ridge

Wanna Munna Flats

Opthalmia

KUNDERONG RANGE

24°

120°

Mt Channer

Limerick Hill

Dublin Hill

WITTENOOM

Mt George

Marandoo

Marnina Gorge

Wittenoom Gorge

Watkins Gorge

Bee Gorge

Hancock Gorge

Kalamina Gorge

Yampire Falls

Fortescue Falls

Mt Vigors

Mt Bruce

Mt Frederick

Mt King

Mt King Gorge

Rio Tinto Gorge

Wittenoom Gorge

Fortescue River South

Turee Creek

HAMERSLEY RANGE NATIONAL PARK

HAMERSLEY RANGE

Mt Windell

Mt Barricade

Juno Downs

Mt Meharry

Mt Robinson

The Grovenor

Coondewanna Hill

Padtherung Hill

Mt Trevarton

Mt Bennett

Turee Creek East

Turee Creek

Tunnel Creek

Turee Creek

Snowy Mountain

Angelo River

Savory Creek

About the authors

Jack McPhee was born 25th November 1905 in Moolyella in the Pilbara of Western Australia and has lived a full life working throughout this large region. Another account of his life is in the work *Wanamurraganya* by Sally Morgan. He now lives in retirement in South Hedland.

Patricia Konigsberg was born in 1959 in West Germany. She holds a BA degree in General Linguistics, French Literature and has a Diploma in Education. She speaks five languages and has been teaching in Western Australia since 1982. In 1988, she moved to the Pilbara to continue her private research into Aboriginal languages and work at Pundulmurra College, a college for adult Aboriginal people. Bee Hill River Man, Kandulangu-bidi results from her work with Jack McPhee and Nyamal place names and locates them in Jack's traditional country. Patricia now lives in Perth with her husband and her daughter and works at the Education Department of Western Australia.